THE WHITE ISLAND

John Lister-Kaye was born in 1946. After a traditional education he became deeply interested in nature conservation and rejected a planned career in order to help in the formation of the Westbury-upon-Trym Wildlife Park near Bristol. In 1965 he spent a year teaching handicapped children and then joined a family business in Bristol. When that was taken over, he found himself working in PR and Sales for a large international organization. He was sent to South Wales, where he worked in the heart of the steel complex. Appalled by the pollution of the Swansea Valley and the surrounding area, he turned his attention more than ever to nature conservation and began writing about wildlife preservation.

In 1968 Gavin Maxwell drew up plans for a Scottish wildlife park on his Hebridean island and invited John Lister-Kaye to become its curator and organizer and to co-author with him a book on British mammals. This he did until Gavin Maxwell's untimely death in 1969, when both projects had to be abandoned.

Now living in Inverness-shire, John Lister-Kaye spends his winters writing and his summers promoting environmental awareness and the appreciation of wildlife through his tourist organization, Highland Wildlife Enterprises.

JOHN LISTER-KAYE

THE WHITE ISLAND

Pan Books London and Sydney

First published 1972 by the Longman Group Ltd
This edition published 1976 by Pan Books Ltd,
Cavaye Place, London sw10 9pg
© John Lister-Kaye 1972
isbn 0 330 24226 1
Printed and bound in Great Britain by
Hazell Watson & Viney Ltd, Aylesbury, Bucks

Contents

Acknowledgements

The author would like to thank Lilian and Lovell Foot, Geoffrey Newlands, Colin and Clodagh MacKenzie and Ann Collins for their generous help and encouragement.

List of Illustrations

To Stuart Lennox and the surgical staff of
the Brompton Hospital Cardiac Unit

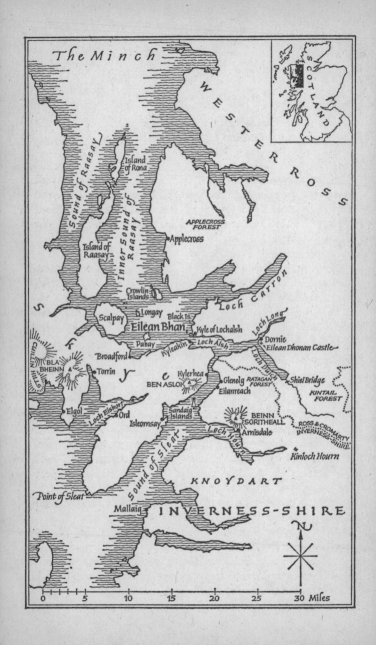

ONE

Escape to the North

When at last I awoke I was aware that the telephone had been ringing for some time. I groped for the light and looked at the clock. It was a ridiculous hour and by the time I had struggled out of bed and pressed the cold receiver to my ear I was cross.

'Swansea 2638,' I snapped.

'One moment please, I have a call for you.' Then silence. The voice vanished diplomatically. Then she was back, this time addressing the source of the intrusion. Extravagant explanations were flashing through my mind : death, fire, accident, when a thin, controlled, infinitely distant voice broke through. 'May I speak to John Lister-Kaye?'

'Speaking,' I replied anxiously, all aggression gone.

'John, this is Gavin Maxwell. Hope I didn't get you out of bed?'

'No,' I lied, 'I often sit up 'til two-fifteen in case the phone rings.' Sarcasm seemed to be my only weapon and I regretted it immediately.

'Is it really that time? I'm so sorry, I had no idea, one loses sense of time up here so easily.' I knew that was true. I had often stayed in the Highlands of Scotland and completely lost track of hour, day and date. I felt deflated.

'I'm sorry Gavin, I wasn't fully awake. It's good to hear from you again. What can I do for you?'

'A lot I hope. You see, I want to compile a book on the mammals of Britain and I need a co-author. I wondered if you'd like to help me write it? It'd mean a lot of work and you'd probably have to come up here so that we could work together. What d'you think?'

'Hey! Hold on!' I expostulated, 'I can't think that fast, I'm still half asleep. A book on what?'

'British wild mammals, all 125 of 'em including aliens. It'd take a long time to get all the existing work together, that's why I need a partner. How about it?' There was a short silence.

'Gavin, I'd love to do this with you but – er – will you let me sleep on it and ring you back tomorrow?'

'Yes, yes, of course. Tomorrow evening?'

'Seven o'clock?' I suggested.

'Right! Fine, ring me then and – er – sorry about getting you out of bed. Cheerio!'

''Bye.' The phone clicked and purred. I replaced the receiver slowly. I found a cigarette on my desk and lit it and pulled on it strongly. I continued to sit by the phone for some minutes watching the smoke curl upwards from the cigarette.

There was no need to delay my decision for even an hour. I had known that I would go before I had replaced the receiver. It was one of those unique opportunities which must be taken regardless of inconvenience or obstacle.

I had known and corresponded with Gavin Maxwell for several years. In 1964 I had joined David Chaffe at the start of the Westbury-upon-Trym Wildlife Park on the outskirts of Bristol, and early in the project Gavin Maxwell had written offering us a tame Scottish otter which had come into his possession. We were ill-equipped to house an otter and we had to decline the gift but contact was made and a little later we were in touch again. This time it was not otters but wild-cats, and with them came Terry Nutkins who had been employed by Gavin to look after the famous Camusfeàrna otters immortalized in *Ring of Bright Water*.

Terry's wild-cats, a tom and a she-cat, had been hand-reared from kittens, but, true to legend, they had matured as wild and unmanageable as the rugged Sutherland hills they came from. But they were a handsome contribution to a new wildlife park and we accepted them gratefully.

A few months later Terry and I travelled north to Camus-feàrna, or Sandaig as was its proper name. It was spring and my first experience of the West Highland Seaboard. After suburban Bristol it was Eden; a paradise undreamed of and it impressed me as it had thousands before me, so that I knew I must return.

With the spring had begun the snow-thaw though there was yet a high cap of snow, pink in the morning sun, on the towering mass of Ben Sgriol. As we twisted and turned our way down the hazardous single-track road from Glenelg to Sandaig, the sound of rushing snow water, dashing from pool to pool as it cascaded down the mountain, was louder than our car engine. In places, the burns broke out over the road in bubbling, sparkling fords so that we had to stop and inspect them before venturing to cross.

That first memory is now confused by many later impressions in every season, but the beauty of the approach cannot be forgotten. I remember that it was early morning and that, as we zigzagged up the road through the thick forestry on Mam Rattagan, we surprised roe deer grazing the grass on the road verge. Our progress was punctuated by their white rumps vanishing into the dark forest as we passed. Later, beyond Glenelg, we found parties of red deer on the road and they scattered before us, stopping at a safe distance to stand and watch us pass, ears up and antlers like branches against the sky.

The road down to the house at Sandaig was never anything but a track, and a track which often proved impassable even to versatile jeeps and Land Rovers. We left our car on the road at the top, and Terry led me down the steep and long footpath, through fresh forestry plantation; sharply down beside the burn, veering left and right to make the descent easier, until suddenly, quite unexpectedly, the whole view of the house, the horse-shoe bay and its chain of islands, lay open before us. What happy memories that view revived in Terry I had to guess, because he broke into a run and a minute later we were crossing the little wooden bridge over the burn almost at sea-level, only a few yards from the house.

At that time Sandaig had very considerably altered from its original primitive state when Gavin Maxwell first occupied it in 1950. Now it had water piped to the house, electricity and a telephone, and sanitation as well as an array of extensions and out-buildings, fences, paling and enclosures for the otters and the menagerie of additional animal life which had somehow accumulated. I remember it as a place of great activity. There were Land Rovers and jeeps, boats and winches; *Polar Star* – Gavin's forty-foot launch – was cradled near the house; and supplies of boots, buckets and rope sufficient to stock a modest ship chandlery. The establishment was capably run by Jimmy Watt, who emerged from the engine well of *Polar Star*, oil up to his elbows, in jeans and a fisherman's jersey and with a broad grin beneath a mop of unintentionally oily hair.

We were there for three days during which we climbed the hills and explored the bay and its islands. Gavin was working long hours to complete a manuscript and we saw little of him by day; but each evening he emerged from his study to join us in the living-room where we talked late into the night over the customary Highland *dram* and to the melancholy moan of the wind in the chimney. I recall the confused impression, shrouded in mystery, of a famous and successful author and a complex man; – little else, I think, revealed itself at that time, but happily Gavin recognized in me an involvement in natural history similar to his own, which in later years broadened into a rewarding friendship.

Later that year I left the Wildlife Park at Westbury to seek my fortunes elsewhere. Three years later my fortunes had certainly changed, but I was far from content. After a brief career in a family business of engineers' merchants in Bristol I found myself caught up in a take-over by a large and uncomfortably distant engineering group of international dimensions. Suddenly the fashionable impersonality of big business was all round me. Overnight someone had swapped my name for a number, and with little less than a week's warning the god whose predictable wrath and pleasure I had come to know was rudely removed to premature retirement at the end of a protracted world-cruise, and replaced by a consortium of demi-gods whose names I could never remember and whose faces I never knew. That identification with one's superiors necessary for the enjoyment of one's work was absent, and in a moment of mental aberration I applied for a vacancy in the heart of industrial South Wales. Distance, I thought, might help. It was a misconception. In the event, the fire proved less comfortable than the frying-pan and, while Swansea was perhaps the least objectionable of the industrial-belt towns, it bore little resemblance to the Somerset village scenes of my childhood.

I moved into the only block of luxury flats Swansea possessed at that time in an attempt to escape from the stacks and towers of the surrounding steel towns. But it was a poor escape. My windows faced east across Swansea bay to the very heart of the steel complex at Port Talbot, and only by sitting in the window and looking south could I exact any sympathy from the grey Channel waters and the distant Exmoor hills, and I could only do that when the double glazing had no mist between its panes. The under-floor central heating cost the earth to run and made the carpet smell and the lino shrink, and the waste-disposal unit jammed when I gave it waste to eat and happily disposed of silver teaspoons, washing up brushes and dish-cloths when I wasn't looking. The walls, however, were sound-proofed and might have been effective had it not been for the air-conditioning duct. The central channel ran the full height of the building like a chimney and from it branched ducts which led to every apartment to extract the stale air. But they also extracted sound, and by standing beside the grille in my kitchen I could hear a dozen voices and the clatter of pots and pans from every other kitchen above and below me. There were other disadvantages too, like the thermostat on the wall in my bedroom; this buzzed like an angry wasp and finally switched on with a thud like a fore-hand drive with a tennis racquet. And there was Joe Hicks. Joe was foreman of the builder's gang who had built the block and, when I moved in, were still working on the garages and paving the exterior. Joe was a Cockney with typical Cockney charm and it was his responsibility to see that every resident was satisfied with his apartment when he moved in.

'Nah don't you worry yerself abaht nuffink, boy,' he had assured me when I agreed to take the flat; 'if there's anyfink as goes wrong, you come an' tell me abaht it, awl right?'

A week later when I discovered that my immersion heater boost switch was not working I went to Joe.

'Not working? Whatcher mean, not working?'

'I don't think the switch is properly wired up,' I explained.

'I knew it! I bloody knew it!' he exclaimed. 'It's those bleedin' electricians again. Don't you worry, boy, I'll fix the bastard what done that switch, don't you worry.'

I waited a month before I approached him again. 'Er . . . Joe, do you remember that switch . . . ?'

'Awl right, awl right, I know. Whatcher think I am, a ruddy magician?' And so it went on.

My second winter in Swansea had been really unpleasant. The autumn of 1968 had been continuously wet, accompanied by clinging sea mists. By Christmas the rain had changed only to sleet driven by knife-edged winds. That it was sleet was bad enough, but its combination with the soot and grime which are a permanent feature of that industrial air, made conditions almost unbearable. By February I had relinquished all hope of winter ever ending. I survived each day only in anticipation of the hot bath at its end and the climb into warm dry sheets. I would not have believed that one telephone call in the middle of the night could have raised me so quickly from the depression of that winter.

At seven o'clock the next evening I telephoned Gavin

Maxwell. The Swansea telephonist asked me to repeat the exchange.

'Kyle Akin,' I said, 'K for King; Y for yellow; L for London . . . And it's an island in the Inner Hebrides and it's connected by radio telephone.' There was a long silence punctuated occasionally by electronic flatulence. Then I heard a distant voice say 'This is Glasgow, try Inverness.' Another pause and more noises, then 'Inverness. What exchange?' Then a longer pause and dead silence. At last the operator came back.

'You're through now, go ahead please.'

Our conversation was brief and to the point. I agreed to travel north at the end of the month to make some detailed plans.

The next ten days were busy. I can't recall why they were busy but they passed more quickly than the previous five and I found no time to grouse about the weather which made no attempt to improve. February ended on a Friday and I spent most of it preparing for my journey. I decided to drive up to Scotland overnight; I had done it before and knew the routine well. I packed a basket of food : cold sausages, veal, ham and egg pie, salmon and cucumber sandwiches, apples and bananas. I put hot soup in one flask and coffee in another, and threw in a couple of cans of beer for good measure. I had been to the Hebrides in March before and I knew how wet and stormy it could be. My suitcase bulged with thick-knit sweaters and stockings and old tweed suits.

I set off in high spirits, humming happily to myself as I often do when driving alone. The rain had eased and visibility was fairly good. Steel works slipped past me; all their stacks and towers sticking up like missiles ready to be launched. Some smoked, others steamed, and the big ones from the blast furnaces belched orange smoke and tongues of flame. The roads there are wide and fluent and cut deep scars across the landscape; they, like everything else there, serve the industry. Even the trees on the hills far above the road have succumbed to the atmosphere. They are just rows of skeletons now, poisoned by that orange, stifling smoke. I looked across the works to the marshes and the sea beyond. Once I had met an old man sitting on the beach there. He had spoken of those marshes :

'Used to be thick with geese and ducks all winter before the steel come,' he had said as he sucked his empty pipe and looked glassily out to sea. 'None there now, not for years, not since the steel come.'

I overtook an enormous wagon carrying two vast ingot moulds with a crust of steel around their lips. I cleared the muck from the windscreen with a squirt of water and drove on up the motorway. There seemed to be no end to the lorries, like worker bees at the mouth of a gigantic hive. Even far out into the Welsh countryside I met them, trundling to and from depot and mill with slag, steaming coke fresh from the coolers, acid and fuel tankers and steel; steel, steel, steel, in rods, tubes, bars, ingots, rolled strip and sheets . . . world without end.

The day began to draw in and suddenly got darker. I swung off the main road and started to climb a twisty mountain lane. For a moment I forgot about steel. At the top of the hill I saw a sign to a friend's farm and turned impulsively down the track. I wound round the muddy puddles and pulled in their yard. The air was full of the barking of dogs. My friends breed gun-dogs and the wire front to the kennel enclosure was suddenly straining with dogs. I could see spaniels and pointers, labradors and setters; springers and cockers, English and Irish, clumbers and cavaliers. I ran down the path to the back door and burst in. The friendly smells of a farmhouse kitchen rushed out at me and the terriers leapt from their basket to greet me.

Llangernew is one of those houses in which it is impossible to feel ill at ease. Goronwy and Bet are a private paradox; they are neither complementary nor supplementary to each other and they exist at odds, but under permanent treaty.

The result is delightful. Neither concedes a point to the other on any score, and as a guest one is extravagantly entertained in duplicate.

Goronwy is as Welsh as his name. He is dark, with a complexion of well-oiled leather, uncompromising as the nails in his boots; Bet is a Scot and displays strong, characteristic patriotism. She is keen and perceptive and incurably romantic beneath a bold exterior. Combined, they produce an invigorating atmosphere.

'God pluck a duck! Look 'oo it is,' said Goronwy standing in his socks in the living-room doorway. 'All the stains come out in the wash.' He chuckled as he beckoned me in.

'Good to see you John,' said Bet getting up as I entered the room; 'sit here while I fetch you a cup of tea.'

'Thanks Bet,' I said, and I sat down by the glowing fire.

'Well, how's the business world?' asked Goronwy.

'I'd swap it for your life any day,' I answered grimly.

'Oh no you wouldn't.' Gron wiggled a pink toe at me. 'I can't even afford a new pair of socks.' Bet came in with a steaming cup of tea.

'Get that in you, boy,' she said with a maternal smile. I sipped the brew cautiously.

'How are the dogs?' I asked, putting the tea down by the fire.

Gron sat up with a jerk. He pointed a gnarled finger at me and exclaimed to Bet:

'Good God, he's just the boy!'

'What now?' I questioned.

'Come out here, boy, an' see what I've got lined up for you.' I followed Goronwy into the kitchen where he tugged on his boots. We crossed the yard and entered a stable. The light flicked on and Goronwy pointed to a heap of straw on the floor of a stall.

'What d'you think of that then, eh?'

A single, white, blunt-nosed labrador puppy blinked at us from the straw. It wobbled towards the voice and I bent down and picked it up. It was a strong, plump puppy of six weeks old and it had big, brown eyes.

The puppy had been selected as best of his litter and had been reserved for a much more stately destination than he would ever share with me. Through no fault of the dog the deal had fallen through and he was temporarily homeless. His pedigree suggested great promise. Field trial and show champions were dotted throughout his lineage and his parents had both been excellent gun-dogs.

'He's a grand pup,' I observed.

'Right, he's yours then,' said Gron decisively.

'Don't be daft, man,' I said. 'How can I keep a dog?' I put the puppy back in the straw. Gron said nothing.

As we crossed the yard to the house I thought about going to live in the Highlands. There would be a wonderful opportunity to raise a dog. I had long wanted a dog of my own but my way of life had always prevented it. I felt myself giving way. Back inside, pressure was re-doubled against me by both Goronwy and Bet. They waved aside my doubts. Within half an hour I had relented and I owned a dog.

'You'll never regret it, boy,' said Gron. 'If you treat him right he'll be taking you shooting in a year's time.'

I agreed to collect the puppy on my way down from Scotland ten days later. Hastily I departed. I wanted to go back for another look at my latest dependant but I satisfied myself with a mental search for a suitable name. I had already lost an hour of travelling time and I sped on into the night anxious to lose no more. Travelling by night meant less traffic and less congestion in the one or two cities I had to pass through. I adjusted my schedule to arrive in Kyle of Lochalsh by ten o'clock the following morning.

Conditions appeared to be improving. The wind had dropped and the rain slackened to a slight drizzle. As I climbed away from the coast, up the treacherous winding road which struggles upwards through hair-pin after hair-pin bend with drops of hundreds of feet on one side and the towering black mass of Rhondda on the other, I glanced back to see the southern sky ablaze with red and ochre fire from the steel works at Port Talbot. How many miles and how many mountains, I wondered, must I put in its path before I was out of range of its strange beauty and power to hurt?

TWO

Fresh Hills and Outer Air

The dawn crept up on me from behind as I drove west through the early morning mist in Glencoe. I pulled into a lay-by and stopped. The silence was sudden and powerful. I got out and looked back. The Grampian peaks were silhouetted in the pale spreading light. I found a flask and poured myself a beaker of hot steaming soup. I stood the soup on the bonnet of the car and stretched : first my arms and shoulders and then my back and legs. After the fug of the car heater the crisp air was good and refreshing. I had made good time and I welcomed the break. Clasping the hot beaker in my hands I walked back down the road to take in the full atmosphere of the glen. I stood for a moment on the wet grass by the roadside recalling the tragic history which, two hundred and seventy years ago, had made these hills so famous. The setting for the massacre was perfect. I wondered how many of the clan Donald were watching from the rugged corries, alert like deer, testing the morning air for danger. Wisps of low-lying mist hung in the windless air, hiding what? A platoon of Argyll's regiment of foot, perhaps? Their scarlet tunics and bright yellow hose conspicuous in such uniform desolation. Their pikes and rifles glinting in the early light. Or Campbell of Glenlyon himself on his grey stallion, his yellow hair delicately groomed to his shoulders, his flushed complexion and heavy arrogant jaw set hard with hatred and revenge? The silence played tricks on my unaccustomed ears. Was that a cough? Or the stamp of an impatient hoof? I scanned the empty moor and pockets of stagnant mist for movement. A thin, shrill whistle cut the silence. Then the buzzard wheeled into sight; a speck against the cloud; high, soaring, its piercing, plaintive cry symbolic at that moment of both the hunter and the hunted.

I stamped back to the car, and drove on up the glen towards Loch Leven.

My mind turned again to the plight of those who had escaped death on that bitter February morning. It must have been colder than this by many degrees, I thought, with the snow deep on the moor and driven by the wind into treacherous drifts on the hill. Those who fled to the hills with John and Alasdair Og, the murdered MacIain's sons, can have found little consolation in their escape when exposed to the gruelling winter conditions. How many gave in to the temptation to lie down in the snow and sleep – and died there, frozen to the ice beneath them? How many, I wondered, had taken weapons to hunt the deer, hares and ptarmigan for food? Can they have dared to light fires to cook and warm themselves with Redcoat patrols scouring the mountains? How many reached the sanctuary of Appin? Time and legend have distorted the facts but there is little doubt that they were hard men in hard times. There can be few sites of historical events so little changed in three hundred years and yet so high on the tourist list : a road and a railway and a few more houses and hotels; but the armies still come, disorderly now in coaches and cars and multi-coloured tunics to shoot their cameras at the MacDonalds who are today as proud of their persecuted ancestry as any of the clans.

Where the road meets Loch Leven it turns sharply left and right. Left to Ballachulish and the ferry and right on a route sixteen miles around the loch to a point on the northern shore not two hundred yards across the water from where it started. I knew that the ferry would not be working at that hour so I turned right to circuit the loch by road. The water reflected the pale grey sky and the dark shadows of its wooded sides.

By seven-thirty the sun was rising into a silver sky, its edges faintly blue. I had left February and the rain behind in

England. I crept through sleeping Fort William and Spean Bridge and sped on up the side of Loch Lochy to Invergarry. Here the new road to the west turns sharply left along Loch Garry and eventually joins the Invermoriston–Kyle of Lochalsh road, the main route to Skye.

I had first motored to Skye five years before and the road in those days was a hazardous single track with infrequent passing places. Now it is wide and straight and the tourist traffic roars along it unaware of the abandoned loops of decaying tarmac which wind away above and below it, ruins of a road and an era. The new road is convenient and fast, but for me the magic of the old track is lost. Seventeen of the peaks along that road are over three thousand feet and their massive grassy slopes sweep upwards from the road on the north and from the loch shore on the south. Slopes so vast that at first the eye cannot gauge the distance until a yardstick is recognized. Sheep are tiny white specks scarcely visible with the naked eye.

I have often heard summer visitors complain that they have never seen the Highland deer although they have searched every open hillside. The reason is simple. Town and city folk habitually restrict the use of their eyes to short and middle distances. Eyes accustomed to focusing on easily identified objects at close range cannot cope with vast open spaces, and perspective is lost. More important is the mental picture. The mental image required to recognize the deer at unfamiliar range is absent through lack of experience. I once helped a man spot some deer on the hill in Cluanie. He had been looking at them for half an hour but had not recognized them. He was expecting to see a definite animal shape and antlers too. The deer I pointed out had no shape, they were minute brown specks. He had no experience of long-range perspective and was astonished when I told him that the deer were over a mile away. Telescopes and field glasses merely complicate the perspective issue. The deer expert finds his specks with the naked eye and checks the details through a glass afterwards.

When the old road first led me through Glen Shiel I was unprepared. The vast expanse of Cluanie had lulled me into false security and when in Shiel the mountains loomed so close and so sheer that there seemed to be no room for the road, I felt insignificant and uneasy. The bulk of jagged rock towering above me I found oppressive and unnerving and it recalled for a moment that childhood image of an enormous stone statue which stood in a park near my home. As children, my sister and I knew him as the giant. He was very big and had folded arms and a bushy beard and, like most stone statues, had no pupils to his eyes which made him look as if he were asleep. Everytime we approached the spot my mother told us to tip-toe past in case we woke him up. Above all we must not laugh, for his anger was so dreadful that we should certainly die of fright. There was something of the awe of our giant about the mountains in Glen Shiel and I crept quietly through the gorge until I was out of their threatening shadow. Several years later when I had become familiar with the road and accustomed to the mountains I saw the wreck of a crushed car lying beside the road at the foot of one of the steepest slopes. A fifteen-hundredweight boulder had toppled from hundreds of feet up and landed on the car roof. I couldn't help wondering whether the unfortunate owner had laughed in mockery at the mountain.

Now, on a bright February morning, my drive was leisurely along the new road and I stopped twice to watch the deer in Glen Cluanie. The loch was milky blue and each mountain was pink-capped with snow in the sunlight. Small groups of deer were grazing their way back to the security of the middle slopes below the snow line, having sampled the sweet grass by the river in the bottom of the glen under cover of darkness. Most of the stags were still wearing the previous year's growth of antlers, but one aged stag I saw had cast both his and he looked foolish and incongruous. His powerful neck supported a head grotesquely out of proportion.

The hinds were distinctly segregated from the stags, many of them in small groups well up on the hill. Some were already lying down and looked firmly positioned for the day. It looked as though they had left the feeding grounds some time before the stags.

It was here in Glen Shiel, one spring morning three years before, that I had seen a small group of stags grazing in a hollow on the other side of the river a mere fifty yards below the road on the south side. This had seemed a good opportunity to take some photographs of Highland red deer in their natural environment, so I drove on round a bend out of their sight and earshot and pulled the car into the side of the road. Armed with a camera, but sadly no telescopic lens, I crept back up the road until I reached a point from which I could survey the lie of the land. The wind was at my back, so, in order to prevent my scent being carried to the deer, I had to circle widely around them and approach from the opposite direction. On the north side of the road a rocky bank rose steeply for thirty feet or more. At the top was a seven-foot deer fence, and beyond rose the hill blanketed for the next thousand feet by dark and dense coniferous forestry. Keen to secure some photographs, I scaled the bank and climbed between the tensioned strands of the fence to enter the enveloping darkness of the trees. I kept the fence in sight on my right as I fought my way along the edge of the plantation for what I estimated to be about two hundred yards on a course roughly parallel to the road. This was a long and laborious business; the trees were closely planted and their lower branches which had not been removed (as is usual forestry practice) formed such an impenetrable barrier that I was forced to make further minor detours to get round them.

Eventually, scratched and weary I arrived back at the deer fence which had now risen to over fifty feet above the road. But the bank at this point was so steep and dangerous with loose stones that I chose to move on down the fence in search of a better way out. I reached the road in safety and crept to a vantage point on its south side. I need not have bothered to creep. My detour had taken me past the deer by nearly a quarter of a mile. In order to approach directly into the wind I had now to climb down to the floor of the glen, cross the river and stalk the deer up the far bank. From the road, the river had appeared to be a gentle flow over a gravel bed well studded with protruding boulders and stones. Seen from its northern bank, its character was considerably altered. The current was strong, sweeping from pool to pool over frequent rapids. There were few places where I could safely cross and none where I could do so dry shod. My mission had by this time cost me too much in time and energy to be abandoned for the sake of a mountain stream, so I boldly stepped into the icy flow. It felt as though all the snow and frost of a thousand mountain slopes were concentrated in this one stream. I waded on until in midstream I was gasping for breath as the water lapped at my waist.

The deer were now hidden from me by a bluff and I crossed the ground to this ridge quickly and without difficulty. Cautiously I crawled up on my belly and peered over the edge. There, only twenty yards below me, eleven young stags were unconcernedly grazing the grass by the river. I thought that by crawling along the hollow I could get to within fifteen yards of the stags on their level instead of being above them; so, waiting for a moment when all their heads were down, I hopped over the ridge and flung myself full length into the few inches of dead ground. An unpleasant squelch greeted my arrival in the bog – for such it was in its most vivid interpretation. My elbows and knees sank into the ooze and its rank pungent stench, so foul that I turned my head away to breathe, invaded every stitch of my clothing and inch of my person. Desperately clutching my camera in my teeth, I crawled for sixty filthy feet while the evil liquid filled my boots and sleeves, and soaked into the wool of my sweater and tweeds. I emerged from that bog like a wart-hog from its wallow.

From a distance of twelve yards, however, still lying on my stomach, I took six photographs of the deer. At the first shutter release the stags were aware of my presence. Every beast was now eyeing me with bovine curiosity, most uncharacteristic behaviour for so timid a species. I was puzzled. Perhaps my camouflage was more complete than I had imagined now that it included shades of bog-water brown. I decided to stand up slowly and photograph their retreat.

The normal reaction of any ordinary wild stag to a dripping apparition arising from the ground at such close range would almost certainly be immediate flight. But these, I quickly discovered, were no ordinary stags. To my astonishment they stood their ground, staring wide-eyed at me with disbelief. My camera clicked and whirred as I took photograph after photograph. I advanced to within eight feet of the nearest beast, a young stag with thin but prettily curved antlers, and photographed him stretching his nose towards the camera. He was no more afraid of me than an amiable donkey. Eventually, they decided that despite my familiar boggy smell I had little to offer them, and they ambled off to graze another patch.

Subsequently, much to my chagrin, I discovered that the forester who lived in a little cabin on the other side of the road had regularly fed the deer on hay and potatoes throughout the winter months when deep snow on the hill prevented grazing. The starving beasts had become so accustomed to being fed at this spot that they were tame enough to take food from the forester's hand. Even though the feeding had stopped with the spring thaw, these young stags still lingered on in greedy expectation.

Now, as I drove past the spot again, I laughed to myself; the river winked and glistened but there was no sign of any deer. I sniffed at my old tweed suit, the same I had worn three years before, and the sweet peat-water taint was still faintly discernible even after many dry-cleanings.

At the head of Glen Shiel the river is spanned at an old fording point by Shiel Bridge, a worthy old arch of rock, hewn by craftsmen's hands from the hills. It is the bridge which carries the road to Glenelg and on to Arnisdale, a road which leads to a legend and belongs to another, more poignant tale.

My route led on, past the bridge, to the shores of Loch Duich where the road edges its way around the water until it meets the confluence of the three lochs, Duich, Alsh and Long. There stands the island castle of Eilean Donan. Of all Highland fortresses this must have the finest aspect. It looks five miles down the length of Loch Duich to Invershiel and is framed in the east by the mountains of Shiel and Kintail; to the west it commands the eight miles down Loch Alsh to Skye.

By half past nine I was in Dornie, with ten miles to go. I wound down the car windows and dawdled along drinking in the fresh salt air. Kyle of Lochalsh was barely awake when I drove through its empty street down to the ferry slipway. I parked the car and walked to the edge of the pier. I had often stood here on previous occasions waiting for one of the old, squat ferries to throb its way across the water and clank its iron gangway down on the concrete with straining hawsers and muffled shouts from the ferrymen. The rumbling diesels are thrown full astern to check its forward progress, and the water is churned into foaming turmoil behind. On these occasions my eyes have been drawn across the water to the picturesque ruin of Castle Moille and beyond to the black, rugged horizon formed by the massive hills of Skye and Raasay; but now all my attention was devoted to a line of low heathery islands straggling across the seaway between Skye and the mainland. At the end of the largest and most southerly island stood a stout, white lighthouse. Not a lighthouse of the arrogant, slender breed common to the southern British coasts, but of stocky Gaelic lineage, of broader base and more solid foundation, built to withstand the wildest Hebridean gale; a sentinel to guide the ring-netters in and out of the Kyle. This was Kyle Akin Lighthouse Island, in Gaelic, *Eilean Bhan*, the white island, and my destination.

Under the lee of the bulk of the island a long, low, lime-whitened house crouched in the only really sheltered position. In the days before the automatic light, when two light-keepers and their families lived permanently on the island, it had been two attached houses built one behind the other; but Gavin Maxwell had them converted into one residence shortly after he bought them in 1963. He had moved there after his famous mainland home, Camusfeàrna, which he described in *Ring of Bright Water*, had been completely destroyed by fire in January 1968. This was now his home.

I edged my car gingerly on to the ferry. The only other vehicle waiting to cross to Skye was a cattle wagon which revved its engines violently and spun its rear wheels on the slippery gangway. The ferry lurched under its weight and the cattle moaned distressingly. Suddenly everyone was shouting directions. Three blue-jerseyed ferrymen were waving their arms wildly, all giving conflicting instructions. The bewildered driver got out to look at the situation for himself. The wagon was half on the ferry and half on the slipway. He climbed back into his cab and leaning out through the open door reversed back on to the slipway. Again the ferrymen started to gesticulate wildly, but the driver took no notice; swearing loudly, he drove at the gangway with alarming speed and swung the cumbersome vehicle diagonally across the ribbed platform. The engine revved, the cattle lowed and shifted restlessly; the ferry lurched, and the wagon was aboard. Fright had made the cattle urinate liberally, and the yellow liquid streamed on to the ferry deck. A barrage of invective flowed from a young ferryman while one of his elderly colleagues dipped a bucket over the side to slosh the deck with sea-water. The gangway heaved up and the obscenities were drowned in the roar of the ferry diesels. Slowly we backed away from the slipway.

It is a curious sensation to sit in a car on a ferry and to turn without touching the steering wheel. The engines throbbing up through the car wheels made it feel as though the car engine were running and I was out of control. I was stupidly trying to steer the vessel with my steering wheel when I realized that I was not alone. A weathered face beamed in at me through the car window. He seemed to think it was all a huge joke. I groped for my wallet.

'Are ye there or back again?' he asked.

'Single please,' I replied, handing him a pound. He wound me out a ticket and thrust my change back through the window.

When I looked up again the ferry was well out into the channel and Kyleakin village was creeping steadily nearer. A herring gull landed on the control house roof and uttered a quiet *yak-yak-yak* for the benefit of anyone who happened to be listening.

I stood at the ferry rail and examined the lighthouse island through powerful field glasses, but there was little that I could see; the ferry vibrations blurred my picture and after a few minutes I gave up. Little did I think that I was being closely scrutinized through a ×40 telescope.

The ferry quickly bored across the seaway and its engines were grinding astern again to slow up for the Kyleakin slipway long before I realized we were that close. Kyleakin, it seemed, was asleep too. The slipway was deserted and I edged off the heaving vessel and on to terra firma. Skye is the largest Hebridean Island and has very varied scenery, but the arrival point at Kyleakin is among the most picturesque. There were three coastal fishing vessels tied up to a timber jetty beyond the ferry slipway, and an assortment of dinghies and smaller fishing boats in the tiny sheltered harbour. The few shops and hotels are new and smart, products of the tourist tide, but around these sit the squat white cottages belonging to a remoter era. In the bright sunlight it was a most harmonious scene and I was happy to creep along the empty road peering into windows and doorways as I passed.

I had been forewarned that the usual procedure for guests arriving at Kyleakin was to locate the only telephone kiosk and phone over to the island to make their arrival known, whereupon a boat would be sent across. I found the kiosk without difficulty and parked beside it. I was now less than half a mile from the lighthouse island and could see it and the house clearly. I entered the kiosk and dialled the number. The response was immediate. A familiar voice reiterated the number I had just dialled.

'Gavin,' I started, 'it's John and I'm at . . .'

'Yes, yes I know. I've got the telescope on you and I can see you clearly. I'll send Andrew across in the dinghy right away. See you in ten minutes, cheerio.'

'Oh . . . um . . . yes, thank you . . .' I stammered, but I was too late; the voice on the other end had gone. I was a little unnerved by the realization that my every move since I had boarded the ferry at Kyle had been closely observed from the island house; it looked so ingenuous too, just a low, white house, not an observatory.

I learned later of a similar occasion when a junior member of Gavin Maxwell's staff telephoned the island from the Kyleakin kiosk to report that he had arrived back from his mission. The conversation ran thus :

'I've just arrived back, will you send a boat for me, please?' Then came the curt reply from the island : 'Yes, I will – when you stop picking your nose !'

I parked the car and walked down to the beach with my two heavy suitcases and a bundle of paraphernalia slung round my neck : cameras, field glasses, light meter, and my haversack – that most valuable accoutrement whose contents have on more than one occasion caused me to be labelled the eccentric naturalist. It is in fact a multi-purpose bag in which I keep all the tools of a field naturalist : collecting bottles and tubes, lenses, polythene bags, string, scissors, forceps and penknife, as well as medical supplies like sticking plaster, bandage, midge repellent, brandy flask and a selection of odds and ends which cover any unlikely contingency : a measuring tape, corkscrew and an envelope, paper and pencil. That old webbing bag has proved its worth many times.

I dumped my belongings down on the beach and sat on a large flat stone to await the boat from the island. The sea was calm and in places where no current ran it lay shimmering like glass. At its edge there was the gentlest movement, tiny wavelets lapping the shingle at my feet. The air was so still that I could hear the hum of the dinghy's outboard engine even before it left the island jetty. It appeared suddenly from behind the island promontory like a mouse from its hole and headed out into the seaway, a speck on the water with a curling white wake peeling away from its bow. The seaway was dotted here and there with little groups of guillemots and gulls which rose hurriedly to settle again well clear of the dinghy's path.

The beach shelved away quickly below me and I could see the transition from the crystal shallows at my feet to the vivid green of deeper water a few yards out. Down there I could see oar-weed and sea-tangle waving, an effortless, sinuous motion. The whole scene was so peaceful that with the warm sun on the back of my neck I was tempted to close my eyes and doze. I stood up and stretched and walked a little way down the beach. The island and its stout white sentry were reflected full length in the shimmering deeps at its foot, and behind it the imposing hulks of Raasay and Scalpay stretched dim and blue to the horizon. The sky was bright blue, the first I had seen for many weeks, and wisps of cirrus cloud hung like tufts of cotton wool. The impression after months of storm and wind ran deep and, although I have now seen this water lashed by a hundred-mile-an-hour gale into raging fury with fifteen-foot waves pounding in savage thunder against the lighthouse, that image of tranquillity remains in my mind.

The dinghy nosed on to the shingle beside me with a crunch and Andrew Scot, dressed in a home-made sealskin jacket, offered a greeting hand and a stout arm to take my luggage and help me climb inboard. Andrew was blunt and laconic and had a mop of dark shaggy hair. We had met before, and beyond a greeting he saw no reason for idle chatter. We crossed to the lighthouse in silence. As we drew into the jetty beneath the lighthouse I realized that the low strip of the island which had been visible from Skye and the mainland was but a fraction of its whole area. Andrew secured the dinghy to her mooring and together we walked up the rabbit-cropped sward to the house.

Outside the house stood a long bench seat and a stout table. Gavin sat at the table, leaning forward with his eye to a small telescope on a tripod. The telescope pointed down on to the water directly in front of the island. I approached the table and put down my cases.

'Hello John,' he said still leaning over the telescope. 'So sorry not to greet you properly but there's . . . aha ! . . . no, damn ! it's a cormorant . . . er . . . as I was saying, there's a bird down there I rather want to see. It's dived at the moment but it should be up any moment now.'

'What is it?' I inquired as I unbuckled my field glasses.

'Well, I only caught a glimpse before it dived, but I think it's a white-eyed pochard. I do want you to see it otherwise no one'll believe me.'

'Isn't that the ferruginous duck?' I asked training my glasses on the water.

'Yes, that's it . . . rare vagrant . . . never seen one here before. Trouble is, with all these cormorants and shags bobbing up and down all over the shop it's the devil's own game to know what's what.'

'Aha !' We exclaimed in unison as a brown duck bobbed to the surface and shuffled its tail from side to side.

'That's him all right, can you see him clearly?' said Gavin.

'Yes, fine . . . well, I could, but he's dived again now.'

'Blast it, yes ! So it has.'

We watched the duck for several minutes as it dived and surfaced until it swam out of sight behind one of the smaller islands in the archipelago. Then Gavin got up from the table and we shook hands.

'Hope you're going to enjoy your stay,' he said warmly.

'Well, if you can keep the weather like this and lay on ferruginous ducks to watch every day you might have trouble getting rid of me,' I said seriously. We went into the house.

The double doors led straight into the main room. It was a study and living-room combined, but it was known as the long room. Forty feet long and twelve feet wide with windows along the east wall, it lookèd out down the seaway between Kyle and Kyleakin. The room was dominated at the far end by an enormous Michael Ayrton, a wax and bone picture in low relief of Icarus falling from the sun with scorched wings. Below this framed work was a large natural stone fireplace, and two long Victorian sofas upholstered in silk brocade stood against the walls on either side. In the centre portion of the room beneath a large plate glass window stood a wide mahogany writing desk topped in red leather with gilt edging. This had been William Wordsworth's desk and was on permanent loan to Gavin. I have always thought of that room as a museum and although many of the 'exhibits' were in everyday use, there were few items which had not some individual curiosity whether by virtue of their age, origin, beauty or rarity. The floor was carpeted throughout in a heavily patterned Indian weave and on top of the carpet were spread skin rugs. There were white and brown sheep fleeces, a goat skin, red and fallow deer hides and a hearth-rug made up from the furs of twenty fennec foxes. Around the walls hung a set of sixteen Thorburn water-colours of British game birds, and beside the fireplace were relics of a former venture, savage steel harpoons which were used to capture basking sharks when in 1945 Gavin started the Isle of Soay Shark Fisheries; a venture which, after years of tribulation and colossal expense, had finally to be abandoned. There were also souvenirs of long visits to Morocco where he wrote *Lords of the Atlas*, the dramatic history of the *House of Glaoua* and the tribes of the High Atlas Mountains : curved Moroccan daggers with jewelled hilts and silver sheaths, and primitive soapstone ware carved and decorated with simple dotted designs by the Berber tribesmen – bowls, boxes, jugs, saucers and ash-trays.

And there was also, inevitably, abundant evidence of his love of natural history. The pelt of an arctic fox hung beside the desk; the mantel shelf was cluttered with pebbles and shells intricately patterned by the serpulid worm; brilliant 'eye' feathers from a peacock's tail; two birds of prey skilfully mounted glared at each other across the room, and the framed fossil imprint of the famous *archeopterix* hung over the doorway to another room. The long room was a room for sitting and looking; it reflected the life of a fascinating man; it was a room thick with the atmosphere of travel and adventure and excitement. I found it difficult to sit there and talk about ordinary, everyday trivialities.

But talk we did, at great length. Much had happened since I had last been to stay with Gavin and that evening we picked over our fortunes and misfortunes long into the night. The Camusfeàrna disaster had been a major crisis in his life. The pitch-pine panelling of the interior had turned the fire into a furnace within minutes. There had been only enough time to snatch up two valuable guns and a manuscript; everything else was destroyed including the famous otter Edal. She had been released into her pen beside the house, but, terrified by the heat and the flames she ran back into her hut and was trapped there as the heat burnt through the cord which suspended the trap-door over her entrance. Only Teko, the other otter, survived. His house was far enough away to escape the fire. The loss of home, otter, and every possession except a handful of things in a London flat had been a devastating blow. That evening Gavin re-lived the whole sickening episode for my benefit. I sat and thought of Sandaig, Camusfeàrna's true name, in the old days; not the really early days of fish-box furniture and primus stoves so brilliantly described in *Ring of Bright Water*; I had not known it or its creator in those days – indeed I was scarcely old enough to read when Gavin Maxwell first went to live at

Sandaig; but the years immediately following the publication of *Ring* (Gavin never referred to his book by its full title), the years of constant comings and goings, of boots and buckets and animals, of the endless crash of the waterfall and the murmur of the sea. Now, two years after the fire, only the burn and the sea remain. Even the charred ruins of the house are gone. A cairn is inscribed to the memory of Edal, the otter of *Ring of Bright Water*, 1958–1968 : 'Whatever joy she gave to you, give back to nature' – and a second flat stone adorned only with sea spurrey and marram.

'And this,' said Gavin, waving his hand around the long-room, 'I have tried to make as unlike Sandaig as possible.' Kyleakin certainly was different, but while the décor and convenient lay-out of the island house contrasted sharply with the incommodities of Sandaig, there was much about the place which echoed, if slightly diluted, the magic of *Ring*.

My ten days on the island were full. We discussed our proposed book in detail until the plans and channels of research we were to adopt had covered a wad of foolscap sheets. But these plans were a fraction of those accumulating in Gavin's prolific brain. The days had been hot; balmy, tropical days which belonged more appropriately to August or September than to March. My precautionary supply of thick sweaters and waterproof shoes remained in their suitcase. We worked outside the house at the long weathered table with the telescope permanently between us. The clear air allowed a breathtaking view down Loch Alsh and with the constant movement of sea-birds across the expanse of water before us it was often difficult to concentrate. But it was here that Gavin outlined to me his dream to replace the cremated Camusfeàrna. Kyleakin Island was to become his own private zoo; an oasis of tame animal life; a park of Scottish mammals and birds to which the tourist and visiting naturalist might come and observe at close quarters a representative selection of Highland wildlife which it would be virtually impossible to see in the wild state. The setting was perfect. There was already a flourishing eider-duck colony on the adjoining island, the other islands in the archipelago were teeming with sea-birds, both common and grey seals frequented the surrounding waters and there were often schools of rorquals, porpoises and dolphins as well as some of the rarer whales and basking sharks to be seen passing up and down the Kyle. There was also a domesticated nucleus : Teko, the surviving otter from Camusfeàrna, was housed in the walled-garden, Hazel and Dirk, Gavin's massive, shaggy deer-hounds lolloped idly about the human precinct; and 'Owl', a hand-reared tawny owl had already been commodiously housed in an aviary on the north end of the buildings.

During those ten days we covered every square foot of the eight and a half acre island. We scrambled over the jumble of strewn boulders along its northern shore, we climbed the craggy cliff faces examining every nook and crevice for suitable lairs and nesting sites, we waded through the reed beds of the island's two marshes and sat waist-deep in the heather on the top of the island working out a fence plan that would be as inconspicuous as possible. Gavin's enthusiasm was boundless and infectious. Formidable snags of every shape and description loomed up to limit the extent of the project, but Gavin over-rode each in turn with an exuberant flourish of his hand and the confident assurance 'Oh! That's all right, we can manage that somehow or other,' so that by the end of my stay I was utterly convinced of the project's potential success and longed to move north and become involved with it.

We compiled a list of some twenty species of Scottish mammals and birds ranging from wild-cats to capercailzie, which we were sure we could accommodate comfortably in enclosures whose terrain corresponded as far as possible to that of their natural environment. Most species we hoped we would be able to procure either already tamed or young enough to tame ourselves. Against each entry on our list we scribbled the names of friends, contacts and other lines of supply. We delved deeply into the multiple problems of food supply. We planned a vast deep-freeze unit in which fish and meat could be stored and, for those predators which would require a proportion of fresh food in their diet, we planned to stock the island with wild rabbits which would also help to control the spread of brambles and keep the sward cropped. We designed an escape-proof rat and mouse breeding unit for the same purpose, and we discussed the installation of zinc-lined feed-bins for grain, bran and similar compounds. There seemed to be no end to our resourcefulness. I had done most of it before in a similar project in England and I was in my element.

Only on the morning of my departure did the fine weather begin to break. The sky clouded and a stiff salt breeze sprang up to ruffle the waters, but by then I could not have cared if it had snowed, I had seen the island for nine sun-drenched spring days, and had been captivated by it and its wildlife. Even if I had stayed on and witnessed the storms which ravaged the west coast during the fortnight that followed my departure, my romantic impression would not have been readily daunted. When I stood again on Kyleakin beach and looked back, I saw the island not as it was, dark and brooding under a menacing sky, its waters flecked with angry white horses before the wind, but as it had been when I had stood there nine days before, the lighthouse reflected full length in the deeps at its foot, and parties of gulls and guillemots paddling idly under a vivid blue sky.

THREE

Creatures Great and Small

Full four months elapsed before I returned, finally, to Kyleakin Island. They were months full of the frustration common to moving house and changing occupation brightened only by Max, my labrador puppy. (I had told Gavin in a moment of misguided inspiration that I would name my puppy after him. Indignantly he had forbidden it threatening that if I did, he would ensure that the first wild goat to arrive for the island zoo would be named Lister. But the damage was done and the name Max had stuck.)

My return to South Wales was like a prison sentence. The day of my release was visible, but interminably distant, a glimmer of light at the end of a tunnel through which I was stumbling conscious only that the glimmer was moving, second by second, minute by dawdling minute, in my direction. The weather seemed wetter and windier, the stacks and chimneys to belch thicker and blacker smoke, and my job the more onerous and futile because its end was so clearly in view. But the evenings, when the day's work was done, were different. I had compiled a long list of books on British mammals to which it would be necessary to refer in our handbook. Every night I hurried back to the flat to spend as many hours as I could keep awake in research for our volume. The log of typed notes and references began to grow and the lists of British Museum references to be checked slowly increased. It was completely absorbing and I was happy to lose myself in the task.

At the other end, on Kyleakin Island, Gavin sat late into the nights planning, scrapping and re-planning the island zoo. At first we corresponded daily, letters often crossing in the post so that we would each have to wait another burdensome day for the answer to our questions. Gavin's patience proved weaker than mine. Within ten days of my return as I sat one night at my desk in the research for our book, the telephone rang. It was Gavin. He had written me a letter that evening but could not wait for the morning to post it, let alone the day or more it would take for a reply to arrive. The subject was trivial but with his keen eye for detail he could proceed no further until it was cleared up. It took seconds only to dismiss it but the conversation rambled on : they had had a storm at Kyleakin and a dinghy had sunk ... Teko, the old otter had had toothache and Donald John, the vet from Skye had had to come over to extract a tooth ... a school of porpoises had passed that day ... a gull had flown into the television aerial in the storm and they were feeding it on tinned sardines ... On and on we rambled, now joking and laughing, now deadly serious, Gavin wincing with vicarious pain as he described the gull's broken wing, the tooth extraction, or some other drama which had filled the island days.

That night was the first of dozens of phone calls. They became a compulsion, a habit which neither of us could forgo. I never went out in the evenings in case the phone should ring, and when I telephoned and found the line engaged I became frustrated and stamped restlessly about the flat. I had no interest in South Wales, the local papers bored me and local news bulletins on the radio meant nothing to me. But any mention of the North of Scotland, any tit-bit of news about the Hebrides or the West Highlands was of sudden and immediate concern. I listened to the late-night shipping forecasts to hear what weather they were getting. Malin, Fastnet, Rockall, Bailey, Faroes and, at last, Hebrides. In April there were long periods of storm, force ten some nights, commonly eight or nine, and I would sit in the dull silence of the flat and imagine I could hear the wind and the waves. Gales which then I would have paid to have been able to stand in, full face on Kyleakin jetty, but which later, in the brute force of reality, sent me scuttling for cover behind bolted doors and drawn curtains.

I would happily have forfeited a month's or even two months' salary to have been able to quit my job and hurry north to Kyleakin. I was living two lives. One, by day, a dreary existence which made the hours drag past interminably slowly; and the other by night, at my desk lost in a scattered mass of papers and cigarette ends, and then over the phone, actual verbal contact with that other world which had captured my whole imagination. Incredibly, during the four months I remained in Swansea, Gavin and I, between us, accumulated a bill of over ninety pounds in telephone calls. In the same circumstances I would happily do it again.

It was a cold, blustery July day when I next stood on Kyleakin beach watching the dinghy chopping her way through the waves to meet me. The hills of Skye towered black and huge behind me and the dull shapes of Raasay and the other islands were scarcely visible through the curtain of tumbling cloud along the horizon. The wind was keen in my face and I licked the salt spray from my lips. I felt all the childhood excitement of returning home, a sudden deep affinity with everything. I knew that this was not an escape into fantasy, but a return to the sort of reality which I had forgotten ever existed.

The dinghy crunched into the shingle below me and Donald Mitchell jumped ashore. Andrew Scot had left Gavin Maxwell Enterprises to join the crew of an Arctic trawler and Donald had replaced him. It is difficult now to imagine that there was once a time when I did not know Donald; indeed he was never a stranger because I had been told about him long before we met, but I do recall the embodiment of a remarkably accurate mental image.

'You must be Donald,' I said, and we shook hands.

'And that must be Max,' said Donald pointing to the puppy who was suspiciously eyeing the boat from a safe distance. We unloaded the car and stowed my luggage in the dinghy. I tucked Max firmly under my arm and clambered inboard. Donald, I quickly learned, was not talkative; he was a young man of pensive mood and eloquent silence and what he lacked in manual dexterity was amply repaid in artistic skills far in advance of his seventeen years.

My arrival on Kyleakin Island for the second time was in very different circumstances. Following a short illness, Gavin had been admitted to hospital in Inverness for treatment and the running of the island and supervision of the construction of the zoo was entirely in my charge.

Max sat unhappily in the bows of the boat as we ploughed into the wind which snatched away the drone of the outboard so that it was scarcely audible. With a stiff breeze and a seven-knot tide against us it was impossible to steer a direct route to the island. We hugged the Skye shore making use of the slack water it provided until we had passed the island and could turn and cross the tidal race with the wind in our favour. It seems ridiculous now to write that at one point in that short journey I thought we were going to capsize before we reached the safety of the island bay. Ridiculous, not because my fears were unreasonable – indeed, had the wind turned us broadside at the wrong moment, one wave could very easily have swamped us to the gunnels – but ridiculous because my fears, like those of a poor rider on a strange horse, were based upon unfamiliarity. Now that I have made that crossing so many times, in dinghies, launches, two-seater prams and forty-foot yachts, in gale and in breathless calm, it seems ridiculous to admit that I was unaware of the protective arm of the lighthouse promontory in the shelter of which we were suddenly becalmed and able to complete the last thirty yards to the island jetty in smooth water.

Construction work on the zoo had begun almost immediately after I had left the island in March, and in the interim considerable progress had been made. Fences had been erected, enclosures marked out and a start made on a gigantic scaffolding structure behind the house which would eventually support aviaries for the larger birds of prey.

Donald showed me round. At least in this field I was not a
novice. I had had painful experience of zoo construction in
the past and I knew exactly how high the standard of work-
manship had to be. Even the tamest badger or fox will find
a weak spot in its enclosure and work on it until it is free;
and, while the problem of escape is not so critical on an
island, it was essential that the enclosures should be strong
enough to keep prey and predator apart. The work was
being done by Willie MacAskill, a retired merchant seaman
who lived on Skye. Willie came over to the island six days
each week and fulfilled the combined duties of builder,
carpenter and general factotum. Donald's duties included
the running of the household, the welfare of the animals, and
assisting Willie whenever assistance was required. It remained for me to plan the lay-out of the zoo, arrange the
supply of materials, and, when the time was ripe, to find and
procure the animals we needed.

Donald took me first to examine my own quarters. Gavin
had allotted me the only other house on the island. It stood
at an angle from the north end of the main house like a
dinghy trailing to the side and to the rear of a larger vessel.
Originally it had been the wash-house for the families of
the two light-keepers who occupied the cottages before their
conversion; latterly, when Gavin first acquired the property,
it had been used to house two wild-cats and had logically
been named the cat-house. Now it had been converted into a
self-contained annexe to the main house, comfortably carpeted and furnished, with central heating, hot and cold
water, and a telephone. It was a fascinating little building of
great character with a magnificent view overlooking the
east bay, the eider island and a mile of water across to Kyle
of Lochalsh. Donald introduced it to me as *The Annexe*
but I decided that it should have a name more worthy of
its individuality, so from the three present alternatives I
selected the cat-house and, translating it into Gaelic,
christened it *Taichat*.

During my four months' absence the nucleus of animals

had multiplied, largely by windfall, and I resolved to spend my first evening introducing myself to each in turn. I went first to Owl. Gavin had explained to me that Owl was a very special owl for several reasons. He had arrived in the care of the Maxwell household at the tennis-ball stage, at which point he was assumed to be a perfectly ordinary tawny owlet. At some earlier stage he had fallen from the nest and had suffered irreparable damage to his left wing. It was clear that he would never fly and so he was adopted and reared as a pet with the certain knowledge that he could never be returned to the wild. It happened that while the owlet possessed, at that time, unknown genetic distinctions, he was conditioned by his unconventional upbringing to accept another far more bizarre peculiarity. Through some literary idiosyncrasy Gavin preferred the Chaucerian word *bridde* to our modern counterpart, bird; thus it was that from an early age the owlet became accustomed to being praised and petted in Chaucerian English. The commonest gambit at feeding time was : *'Ye worthy bridde,'* and after feeding : *'Ye bibledde owl'*, and on return to his aviary : *'Farewell my sweete bridde, min trewe amaride.'*

When I approached the aviary that evening I had momentarily forgotten this pattern and I spoke directly to Owl who was peacefully dozing inside his barrel. 'Hello Owl,' I said, hoping he might remember me from our ten days' acquaintance earlier in the year. The owl displayed no sign of recognition. One eyelid flicked up to reveal a disdainful eye which clearly disapproved of the intrusion.

'How's your Chaucer?' whispered Donald from beside me. Suddenly I remembered, and, clearing my throat I tried again.

'Avoy my worthy bridde! Fy on yow herteless owl, 'tis I youre freende.' The response was electric. The owl sat up with a jerk and advanced along his perch bashfully blinking and whimpering in the most endearing manner. I pushed out my finger and he nibbled at it affectionately.

The other distinction which was not discovered until Owl

was fully fledged was that he belonged to the grey-phase of
tawny owl which although fairly common in parts of the
Continent is very rare in Britain. The standard British tawny
owl has rufous-brown upper parts streaked sparsely with
dark brown, but the grey-phase is almost completely grey in
place of rufous-brown, with the same dark brown streaks,
giving the appearance of very smart morning dress.

I bade Owl a Chaucerian farewell and moved on to inspect a temporary pen which had been hurriedly erected to
house a blue mountain hare. But the hare's athletic ability
had been seriously underestimated and as soon as no one was
looking it had hopped out to roam the island at will. This
pen, situated in a sheltered position up against a low cliff
directly behind the house, had remained empty for some
weeks before being used to contain five fledgeling herons
which had been unexpectedly brought to the island. It was
eventually intended to fence off an entire sheltered bay
which lay on the southern shore of the island behind the
lighthouse so that pinioned birds like herons and waders
could dabble around among the rock-pools of the intertidal zone at their leisure. This arrangement would facilitate
feeding problems and would place these captive birds in their
own highly specialized environment. The advent of the
young herons, however, preceded the fencing of this bay and
they had been put, for the sake of convenience, in the hare's
empty pen. There they stood, hunched and incongruous in
the heather, like five grey archdeacons with expressions of
abject ecclesiastical penury. Only at feeding time did they
show any sign of life. As Donald and the fish-bucket approached they fidgeted and chattered amongst themselves
with outstretched necks and impatiently clacking bills.
Herons, like geese, are great alarmists, and at a later date
we discovered that it was advantageous to have them
situated close to the house. No prowler, animal or human,
could approach the buildings without arousing cacophonous
warning from the herons.

Next we visited the foxes. Four cubs had been taken from

a local lair and brought to the island in May at about a month old. They arrived in the delightful chocolate brown, snub-nosed, fluffy stage which all fox cubs go through; and although they were wild and very frightened at first, they quickly became used to being handled and lost their fear of humans. At this crucial stage, unavoidable circumstances removed their keeper and a period elapsed when they were regularly fed but were not handled at all. When Donald arrived as their new keeper, he attempted in good faith to start re-handling them but they savagely resisted him. Now, at four months old they could hardly be called cubs and were certainly not tame.

It was our ideal that all the animals in the collection should be quite unafraid of human approach and, if possible, handleable by one or more members of the staff. Since the conventional zoo principle of concrete cages was unacceptable to us, and because we planned to provide extensive natural cover for every species, it followed that any animal which was at all timid of human approach would promptly take advantage of the cover and hide, thus defeating the object of putting the animal there in the first instance. I stood at the wire of the foxes' pen and considered their plight. Three of them cowered in the concealing gloom of their den, three pairs of wild, darting eyes; and the fourth, a thin, agile vixen with a sharply pointed nose and sandy coloured coat, had already developed the pitiful symptoms of a neurosis common to caged predators. Back and forward she ran, up and down the length of the run, ceaselessly, from end to end, springing up against the timber supports at either end, twisting back and running nimbly to repeat the process with pitiful exactitude, over and over again.

'One of them does seem to be tamer now than when I arrived,' Donald said hopefully. I looked at him and saw no conviction in his eyes. 'No,' I said, 'they'll never get any tamer now, it's too late. They're never going to be happy in captivity and it would be kinder to destroy them.' We turned away from the pen and walked back to the house. I had decided that a less drastic course of action might be to release them quietly at dusk one evening on some remote mountain-side on the mainland, as many miles from human habitation as possible. But my plans for their release were unnecessary. It appeared that my final words as I stood beside the pen had been clearly understood. By morning the foxes had fled. They had found a loose board in the floor and worked at it until they could dig their way out. One problem was solved at least for the time being, but four wild foxes running free on the island held many far greater problems in store for us.

There was also a carrion crow. Crowlin had been so chris-tened by Donald because his aviary, again a temporary but adequate structure, overlooked the Crowlin Islands which lay some six miles to the north-west. Unlike the foxes, Crow-lin was the definitive happy bird. Happier even than his wild scavenging cousins, the ubiquitous 'hoodies', who cawed with hungry frustration outside the wire of his cage while Crowlin, replete and content, brooded over his hoard of carrion delicacies. Crowlin had everything and feared noth-ing. He had full powers of flight, a truly rasping, mocking voice which he put to very good use, the privacy of his den wherein were hidden many secrets, and the security of the friendship of man. He was too young to know about female crows and anyway, so acute were his powers of perception that he was probably well aware of our plans to secure him a wife at a later date. Crowlin was a great asset. He was exactly the sort of bird we wanted. He was very tame and had great character, but I was not keen that he should be allowed freedom of flight around the island. It was certain that little would escape his predatory eye and I feared for the safety of the eider ducklings and the young of any of the small wild birds which might have nested on the isle.

Standing apart from the other animals on the island, aloof and segregated in a private world of fame and stardom, was Teko, the elderly and distinguished otter, the last of Gavin's famous African otters. Teko was old and grumpy and toothless and he lived in absolute retirement, appearing only to feed and cruise gently round his pool as the mood required. He had not taken kindly to the move from Camus-feàrna and on two occasions he had made determined attempts to return to his former home. Now he spent his days curled up in the seclusion of his centrally-heated house – a pig sty which had been specially adapted to suit his needs – from where he hissed at strangers and yikkered defiance at any attempt to call him out.

To me Teko remained, during the short period the Almighty allotted our acquaintance, an enigma. I was unable to analyse the intent behind his peering, myopic gaze. I knew that he had turned on his keepers in the past and had inflicted serious damage. Despite his apparent toothlessness, I was mistrustful and tense on the few occasions that I handled him. I was afraid and he sensed it, and I was the more afraid because I knew he sensed it. My respect for the teeth of any of the mustelines is not based on cowardice but upon experience of which even the memory is painful.

In early adolescence when my natural history studies were fired by a besotted devotion to any furry animal, I discovered the nocturnal delights of badger watching; an illicit involvement with the natural world so much heightened by moonlight and the thrill of breaking bounds that I pursued it throughout my schooldays, and in so doing, I first experienced the relentless tenacity of a wild badger's jaws.

I was well practised in my escape routine. I wore a uniform of black, the hackneyed outfit of the screen cat-burglar: black sweater, black jeans, black plimsolls and gloves, and an old pork-pie hat which, if not quite black was dark enough to suit my purpose. I slipped stealthily out of the dormitory and down a short corridor to the head of an old wooden staircase which led me down three storeys to the ground floor. Each stair was worn smooth by years of careless feet, and I remembered that it was important to tread close to the wall and to take two stairs at a time in order to halve the number of creaks. From the bottom of the stairs the rest was easy, and within seconds I was carefully lifting the cumbersome brass latch of an outside door. The heavy door swung in towards me and I felt the thick night air warm on my face. I recall that it was one of those sticky July nights when the air seems to be composed of 98 per cent midges and 2 per cent bats. The moon was full and bright and made my torch unnecessary. I crept over the gravel terrace and down the steps which led to the tennis-courts. I could feel the accumulated heat of the day flooding up from the tarmac as I passed. Beyond the tennis-courts lay the tree-line, and beyond that, 700 acres of rambling undercliff. My school was situated on a South Devon cliff top, 500 feet above the sea, and the densely wooded undercliff, in parts steep and in places gently shelving in a series of slipped plateaux, besides being school property was a National Nature Reserve and abounded with unmolested wildlife in every form. During the six happy years I was there I attained an intimacy with those woods and cliffs which I have not reached with any other place in the years which have elapsed since I left school. I knew them by day and night and in every season.

My destination that night was the coniferous wooded side of a valley which ran obliquely down to the shore about a mile from the school. There had been a badger colony in this wood for hundreds of years, and their presence was clearly marked by the enormous heaps of sandy soil outside the sett entrances, earthworks which had accumulated over centuries of excavation by the badgers. I was no longer restricted by the precautions necessary for seeing these timid animals. I had visited this colony so frequently by day and night over four years that they had become well acquainted with my scent and were no longer wary of my approach. I knew very well that, provided I arrived by my usual path and climbed into one of my three strategically placed tree-seats, the badgers would reappear within minutes, fully aware of my presence, and continue about their business unperturbed.

That night, however, I never reached my destination. As

I crossed the stream at the bottom of the valley and started to climb the steep bank which led up to the wood, I heard a thrashing sound coming from the undergrowth some distance to my right. At first I thought I had disturbed a small party of roe deer and that they were crashing away in alarm, but the sound persisted and grew no less in volume. My second thought was that a badger was tearing up bracken fronds to take back to its sett for bedding, an endearing characteristic of these animals. But again I was puzzled by the urgency of the sound. I paused to listen more intently. Beyond the thrashing noise was another sound, the strained, anguished, grunting of an animal in pain. I turned and ran back down to the stream and followed its soft gravel bed along past the badger's habitual drinking place until I was directly below the source of the sound. It had stopped and the night was calm and still. I was certain of its approximate location, so I struck uphill fighting my way through the brambles until suddenly the thrashing started again, this time with a renewed, frenzied intensity, only a few yards in front of me. I knew what it was : I even thought I knew which badger it was, and tears foolishly welled up in my eyes to blurr my vision and complicate my task.

I had found snares set to catch badgers before; thick, many stranded wire nooses suspended over their well trodden paths. 'Set for foxes, sonny,' the farmer had told me; but I knew better, and I had returned by night and wrenched their long iron stakes from the ground and hurled them into the sea with all my might. Here was one I had not found, and in it, with the noose biting deep into his flesh was one of my badgers.

When at last I reached the spot I was so horrified by the sight, so furious with the culprit and so filled with pity for the badger that common sense and reason deserted me. The snare had been carefully set just inside a bramble thicket where the badger path became a tunnel, and the beast would have to pass through the noose since there was no way round it. This is precisely what had happened and the badger, a young boar, one of the previous years' cubs from a sett I had watched throughout that summer and knew well by his still fluffy coat, had passed his head and shoulders through the noose until it had tightened around his belly. I estimated that he could easily have been in that noose for four or even five hours. He had probably emerged at dusk and had taken that path down to the stream to drink, since it was a hot night, stopping in at another sett on the way. His violent, frenzied struggles to free himself had pulled the noose so tight that it was constricting his middle to a circle some four inches in diameter; and the wire was so twisted and gnawed by his constant writhing attacks upon it that there was no longer any freedom of movement in the noose. It was drawn as tight as his body would allow, and was now permanently fixed in that hideously constrictive position. The other end of the wire was shackled on to a short length of chain which in turn was attached to a two-foot angle-iron stake which had been driven its full length into the ground. The badger had thrashed his way round and round that pinioning stake, as a tethered cow grazes in a circle; but as there was no swivel on the stake, the wire had twisted tighter and tighter. The entire bramble bush had been completely flattened and bare shredded stalks protruded from the ground where he had savagely attacked anything within his reach.

I removed the red filter from my torch and turned its yellow beam on to the badger. The moonlight had not revealed colours and I winced with horror at the blood which my torch lit up. The entire circle was spattered with blood and saliva. The jagged ends of the gnawed wire had lacerated the badger's tongue and gums and he had broken his teeth on the sharp, hammer-bruised end of the stake. His throat, shoulders and back, where he had turned to bite at the noose, were matted with blood. As he lay on his side heaving with exhaustion, his little pig-eyes stared up at me appealing, I thought, for help.

It did not occur to me at that moment that the badger might not recognize my motives, and, transferring my torch to my teeth, I knelt beside the beast and began to unravel the wire. In a flash, and before I had time to realize what was happening, he had whipped round and savaged my left hand, released it and buried what remained of his broken teeth into my forearm. With a cry of pain I wrenched my arm from the badger's jaws. I felt my flesh tear away with the shirt and pullover, and the hot blood flow down my arm and into my palm. I had dropped the torch and as I groped for it amongst the brambles I recall feeling hurt not at my wounds but that the badger should have so savagely spurned my help. My adolescent powers of reasoning in those circumstances can have been little better than those of the badger because, apparently not content with the vicious bites I had already received, I returned for more.

I can only marvel now that my hands were not seriously and permanently maimed on that occasion. Few people of my acquaintance who have been bitten by adult badgers have escaped without the loss of even one finger. At the time I thought it better not to examine my left hand and forearm; and since the pain was, as yet, numbed by shock, I replaced the torch in my teeth and made a grab for the glowering badger. I managed to get hold of the scruff of its neck with my right hand, and, holding its head firmly to the ground I knelt over it anchoring it securely between my knees. It was becoming difficult to tell which was my blood and which the badger's. The hair on its back was so clogged and matted with blood that a little extra of mine cannot have made much difference. At length I unwound the final twists which locked the noose in so tight a grip, and felt it slacken under my hands. The badger felt it too and renewed his struggles with such a burst of strength that I was barely able to hold it even with my whole weight pinioning it to the ground. As it quietened, I began again to unknot the snare. Finally, after several minutes of twisting, bending and tugging, the wire broke and I gently unthreaded the noose. My forearm and left hand were now extremely painful and I was restricted to the use of only my fore-finger and thumb on that hand. I placed my right hand on the badger's neck, pressed heavily down while I stood up carefully, then sprang away as I released him. He raised himself unsteadily as if unwilling to believe he was free, then turned and shambled off into the undergrowth. The circulation to his hind quarters must have been seriously impaired; he dragged his hind legs, half limping, unable to co-ordinate them with his powerful forepaws which pulled him away into the darkness. I never saw him again although I watched every likely sett for many nights. I suspect that he died of internal injuries, deep underground curled up in the friendly, sweet-smelling warmth of a chamber filled with bracken bedding.

Happily, my own injuries were only superficial and although they were very painful I was able to get back to the school buildings without further incident. The sanatorium matron, a young woman of infinite compassion combined with feminine charm (and, consequently, the unrequited passion of many boys), was a good friend and I went to her early the following morning. She frowned deeply as I unwound the blood-stained handkerchiefs from my arm and hand. In silence she carefully removed the remains of a fingernail and stitched and bandaged my arm. She then gave me an anti-tetanus injection. I thanked her and, as I picked up my jacket to go, wondered what she would say in the sick-list report to my house-master.

'Right then, off you go,' she said, smiling, 'and be careful not to fall on any more broken bottles.'

Today small white scars now scarcely visible bear witness to this experience, but the lesson left a much bolder imprint. It is now only with extreme caution that I handle wild animals, and Teko's senile jaws I held in great respect.

The north-eastern quarter of the lighthouse island is a two-acre promontory separated from the bulk of the island by a diagonal rift which joins two bays on the north and east shores. This valley is boggy and thick with cotton-grass and rushes, but the promontory which rises thirty feet above it is, like the rest of the islands in the archipelago, a rugged volcanic boss largely hidden by heather-covered deposits of peat with its wind and sea worn edges smooth and bare. Willie MacAskill had erected a stout stock fence to enclose this promontory and resident within it were a pair of goats. They were hardly 'wild' as the word is used in this book, but neither could they be called domesticated. There exists, in fact, some doubt as to their origin. There are among the wilder, more desolate uplands of Britain and its islands a number of herds of goats which are almost certainly not indigenous but are feral escapees from domesticity. In such instances they resort to the highest and most inaccessible craggy peaks and very quickly adopt the timid, sure-footed guise of true mountain goats. There are such herds in the Cheviot hills, the Northumbrian fells, the Welsh mountains and in many parts of the remote Western Scottish Highlands and islands. The natural habitat of the wild goat is the high, dry and rocky mountain top and in some regions goats have been intentionally released from domesticity to inhabit and dominate the sparse grazing such heights provide, thereby confining the sheep to lower, more easily accessible ground. Thus it is certain that if in fact any of our truly indigenous mountain goats survived into recent history in these areas, they are now thoroughly interbred with feral escapee or released stock.

Our island goats, a billy and a nanny, were typical of the feral herds. They had long, shaggy, predominantly chocolate brown coats with some creamy white on their throats and bellies; a black tail over a cream rump presented a rear target very like that of a scruffy fallow deer. In other ways too were they true to their kind. On a hot day it was unwise to pass downwind of either of them, but particularly of the billy. Their smell, fetid under normal conditions, became rank in the heat, and what stench the billy achieved in rut I fortunately never experienced. Nevertheless, they were effectively representative of Scottish fauna and by that alone were justly qualified to appear in our collection. Gavin had obtained them locally and brought them to the island before my return, but he had fortunately overlooked his threat and both animals remained unchristened beyond Bill and Nan.

Apart from these few captives the domestic animals included only the dogs, Dirk and Hazel, the two gigantic deer-hounds which, like Teko, had been brought to the island after the Camusfeàrna fire, and a ram. A very handsome ram, but somewhat cramped in his masculine role by the absence of even a single ewe. He also had no name; he accepted his enforced celibacy without protest, and grazed the island in undistracted leisure. Mostly he spent his days within the vicinity of the house and buildings since it was there that existed the only area of open grass on the whole island. I think, too, that he felt some association with the humans and liked to watch what was going on.

I knew very well that the lighthouse island was said to be haunted. In the chapter on Kyleakin in Gavin's book *Raven Seek Thy Brother* the several stories and legends, old and new, were related in detail and when I had first stayed on the island we had discussed the subject at some length. There existed a pattern common to all the stories including the experiences of Richard Frere, Gavin's friend and colleague who had lived alone on the island for some months during the conversion of the two lighthouse cottages in 1965 : it was of muted mutterings and whisperings in some indecipherable tongue rising and falling in intensity and coming from outside the house, but always heard from within. The mutterings were usually followed by loud metallic clanging suggestive of clashing broadswords and claymores. Although I have still never actually heard any of these sounds I have always thought that they fit logically what is known of the history of local events. Tradition has it that Kyle Akin is named after the Norse King Hakon who, according to the Hakon Saga, visited these waters in 1263. Alternatively there is the older tradition that the name arises from Acunn, brother of Riadh (who is said to have given his name to Kyle Rhea, the straits between Skye and the mainland at Glenelg), both Fingalian heroes of the third century, some thousand years before the time of King Hakon. Whichever the case, and both seem likely, there is little doubt that there were raids on or around the island. The obvious course of action by the captain of a hostile longship intent upon looting the Gaelic settlements at Kyle of Lochalsh and Kyle Akin would be to approach stealthily by night, land a warparty on the unsheltered and probably unguarded west shore of the island, and then use the island as an easily defendable headquarters from which forays could be made to pillage the surrounding settlements on Skye and the mainland. It also seems likely that if the islands were inhabited by one or more families during those dark years, their primitive dwellings would have stood on or about the site of the existing lighthouse cottage, since it occupies the only really sheltered situation on the whole island. Ever since I first visited the island I have had a mental picture of the origin of the haunting : of the Viking longship hove to off the island and the Norsemen wading quietly ashore by moonlight, scrambling over the rocks and crouching in the heather on the top of the island overlooking the cluster of small turf-roofed huts below them. Perhaps it was the goats shifting restlessly about the hut's earth floor which stirred a Highlander from his bunk, perhaps a sense of danger in the air that caused him to step outside to see for himself only to come face to face with the Viking gang and to be cut down with a cry of terror where he stood. And then the *mêlée* which followed : savage yells from the Norsemen, screaming women, wildly bleating, stampeding goats and sheep and the clash of arms as the Highland menfolk rushed to the defence of their families.

It was in full consciousness of some such fanciful explanation that I prepared for bed on my first night in Taichat. I drew the curtains tightly across the windows and lit a candle beside my bed. I heard Donald whistling to the deerhounds outside and then his clear voice : 'Are you ready for lights out?'

'Right ho!' I shouted back as I climbed into bed and settled Max on his blanket at my feet. The generator faltered

and the electric lights flickered and faded. The candle cast a
pale oasis of light over the bed and the rest of the room was
plunged into darkness. I heard Donald pass back along the
path to the house and saw his torch beam flash across the
windows.

'Goodnight,' I called, but I had forgotten how brisk was
the wind and my voice escaped unheard. I blew out the
candle, pulled the sheets up under my chin and lay back on
the cold, fresh pillows. Slowly, hesitantly, the pale blue of
the night crept through the gaps between the curtains until
I could make out the exact shape of the windows. The old
fireplaces had been blanked off but the wind still moaned
quietly in the chimneys and a draught shifted the curtains
uncertainly. I was tired after a long journey the previous
night and a full day. Max's deep, orderly breathing suggested that he was already asleep, and as my mind clouded I
remember hearing the shrill piping of oyster-catchers as they
raced overhead in the wind. Then sleep. Deep, soothing sleep
for two, perhaps three, hours.

Suddenly I was wide awake and sitting up, Max somewhere beside me uttering a deep throaty growl. I put out my
hand and felt for him in the dark. He was rigid and trembl-
ing and as I ran my hand over him I felt the hair erect along
the ridge of his back; but I could neither see nor hear anything. Cautiously, ever so carefully I began to feel along the
bedside table for my torch. The candle, the flex of the electric
lamp, a box of matches took shape under my fingers and
then, at last, the cold cylinder of the torch. I felt for the
switch, aimed the tube diagonally across the room to the far
corner – and pressed. The beam shot out from my hand as I
flashed it nervously about the room. To my enormous relief
there was nothing. Then, just as my pulse began to return to
normal, there was a tremendous crash against the door which
I could see give visibly under the impact. Max's rumblings
reached a new intensity and I sat transfixed with the beam
on the door latch expecting at any second to see it fly up
and the door swing open to reveal the Viking, huge and fair,

wet leather and steel glinting in the moonlight. Suddenly, with a snort and a shuffle outside, there was the sound of hooves pounding away from the door. As Max advanced barking furiously I realized who our intruder had been : it was Ram, whose insatiable interest in our affairs had driven him to make this midnight call.

FOUR

Halcyon Days

The early days passed quickly. Life on an island, however modern and well-equipped the living conditions, is essentially different. Above everything is the feeling of separation from the main body of civilization. In no part did that island belong either to the mainland community at Kyle or to Skye. It was separate, individual and aloof. The entire absence of every form of compulsion from any organizing establishment, and of every imposition of routine which one accepts as normal in a communal existence, was something I was not accustomed to, and it took a conscious effort to acclimatize myself. The island was well equipped for long periods of storm when it might not be possible to get a boat into or away from the jetty. The deep-freezes were well stocked with food and there were capacious fuel storage tanks which meant that daily trips to Kyleakin village, although often desirable, were not strictly necessary. In the event, it was found more convenient for Donald to cross to Skye every morning to collect Willie and again at night to take him back than to provide a separate dinghy for Willie's own use. While under different circumstances I would have been content to exist in a state of utopian isolation for days or even weeks at a time, it was clear that in order to get the construction of the zoo under way, some semblance of routine would be necessary. But it was a routine which was happily flexible and which destroyed none of the relaxing benefits of island life.

During those early days I underwent a complete mental reshuffle. For the first time in my adult life I found myself able to review a situation unhindered by considerations of position and status, to be idealistic without fear of scorn or rebuke, and to respond naturally to the demands of an existence free from pretence and devious motivation. I believe that only on an island like Kyleakin is it possible to experience this sort of entire reassessment of purpose and direction. The isolation must be monastic; and the distractions, if there must be distractions, must come not from human intervention but direct from nature.

Our routine was simple and straightforward. We arose as early as the day allowed. On bright fine mornings we were up with the sun and breakfasted on thick pin-meal porridge and toast sitting outside the house. Breakfast in sunglasses and shirt-sleeves I had only previously experienced on the Adriatic; but this was better. There were breathless, shimmering mornings when the sun pounced out from behind the mountains and caught the emerald water before us in a calm so still that the plop of a diving cormorant a hundred yards out was as clear as the chink of our spoons and porringers. Often there would be time to kill before Donald had to cross to Kyleakin beach to collect Willie and, as we waited for breakfast, this would turn into a casual bird-spotting exercise. The telescope was always beside us on the table, and over endless cups of rich Costa Rican coffee we spied on the little groups of guillemots or gulls, eiders or cormorants which were nearly always to be seen. Donald was an experimental ornithologist and his lack of experience was made up for by colourful description which usually completely concealed the identity of the bird. He would return from an errand agog with news of a discovery. 'I've just seen a bird flying across the water. I *think* it was a woodpecker,' he would declare.

'Why do you think it was a woodpecker?' I would ask tentatively.

'Because it looked like one.'

'There aren't many trees round here.'

'It was migrating . . .'

'Oh! Yes, of course.'

'. . . and it made a noise like a woodpecker.'

'Have you ever heard a woodpecker call?'

'No, but it made the sort of noise I would expect a wood-pecker to make.'

'What sort of noise?'

'A noise a bit like some ducks make.'

'Do you think it could have been a duck?'

'Well, yes I *suppose* it could . . .' And so on, round and round : woodpeckers, ducks, divers, thrushes and, as often as not, back to woodpeckers. But it was good practice and slowly, as the days slipped by, Donald became noticeably less extravagant in his descriptions and more and more familiar with the wide assortment of land and sea-birds around us.

Sometimes there would be other far more exciting visitors like a school of whales, rorquals or porpoises; and one morning a young basking shark cruised into the island bay below the house just as we were finishing breakfast. Basking sharks are common in Hebridean waters throughout the summer months but they seldom came into the Kyle straits. Unlike the whales which in size and general appearance they re-semble, sharks are fish, not mammals, and are easily identi-fiable by the large, black, triangular dorsal fin which in an adult shark protrudes from the water by as much as three feet. When basking just below the surface a second fin ap-pears some twelve to twenty-five feet behind the dorsal, de-pending upon the age of the fish; this is the top of the shark's vertical tail (all the whales have horizontal tails) and it waves slowly from side to side as the beast glides smoothly through the water. No other shark or whale has two fins visible at the same time, and only a bull killer whale sports a dorsal fin as high and that is unmistakable by its pointed, sabre-like appearance, acute and short based.

Basking sharks are virtually harmless. They feed on plank-ton, a collective term for all the thousands of minute, free-swimming, plant and animal organisms in the sea. The only danger likely to arise directly from these enormous fish is that a small boat or canoe may be capsized or damaged by the fierce lashing of its tail if the beast is disturbed or frightened. The shark which visited us that morning was no more than twelve feet long and appeared to have chosen our bay in which to bask. The time was approaching ten o'clock when Donald went off down to the jetty to prepare the dinghy for the morning crossing. I stayed and watched the shark through the telescope for a few minutes, then decided that it might be fun to take a closer look. I ran down to the jetty and arrived just as Donald was casting off. 'Hold on!' I shouted and jumped into the bows. 'Let's go round and take a closer look at Sharkie.' The outboard burst into life and we bored out into the Kyle.

As we approached the black triangle, still in the same spot, Donald throttled the engine down so that the vibrations wouldn't frighten the shark away. The water was shallow and clear in the bay and I could see the cumbersome proportions of the beast vividly. It was not black, but a mottled dogfish brown and, as we passed over it, to the rear of its dorsal fin, its whole length quivered with power and it submerged leaving a swirl of churned water in its wake. Thirty seconds later the fin reappeared a few yards to our right. We hurried about to approach it again from the rear. I was fascinated by this leviathan, and, like a child who has been attracted to something, I wanted to touch it. I picked up the boat-hook from the floor of the dinghy, and, holding it aloft like a primitive harpoon, I jabbed ferociously at the shark as we passed over it for the second time. My lunge connected squarely at the base of the fin and it felt like prodding a gigantic, solid door-mat. The fin disappeared and a full two seconds elapsed before the great flailing tail broke the surface beside the boat showering water high into the air, drenching us both, as the shark dived. After that, it was wary of our approach and never allowed us near it again. It repeated its submerging and reappearing tactics with monotonous regularity until we became bored with the game and headed back to the jetty. Our hostility, however, had not deterred it from its purpose because it remained in the close vicinity of the island all day.

On another occasion our breakfast was interrupted by the appearance of a small, opaque, balloon floating past on the morning tide. We watched it for some minutes through the telescope and I knowledgeably identified it as a Portuguese man o' war. These curious animals are often wrongly classified as jelly-fish, but are in fact a complicated colony of individual marine animals, some of which make up the feeding section of the community, some the reproductive, some the attacking and defensive sections, while others produce a gas-filled bag which floats on the surface of the sea and acts as a sail to effect movement. Beneath this bag are suspended a mass of other organs in the shape of tentacles which may extend vertically down for several feet. The sting cells in some of these tentacles are extremely poisonous and have been known to cause human death. Normally these animals live out in the open Atlantic, but after prolonged periods of strong south-west winds they occasionally crop up in quite large numbers on British coasts. I had not heard of their incidence in the Hebrides, so I was keen to make a positive identification. I collected a butterfly net and a bucket, and we chased out in the dinghy to capture our prize. The tide was ebbing fast. The little bag had been carried far out into the Kyle and it took some minutes to overtake it. All this time I was preparing a mental report which I would phone over to the Kyle police following our discovery. I visualized warnings on the local radio and in the local press advising people, especially children, not to touch these extremely poisonous animals. It came, therefore, as something of an anti-climax when, as we drew alongside, I found it to be a very ordinary polythene bag which someone had blown up, knotted and thrown into the sea. My excitement, however, was partially restored when on retrieving the balloon I discovered a slip of paper inside it with the following message :

'FEMALES BETWEEN THE AGES OF 16 AND 25 PLEASE CONTACT J. R. TAYLOR, TEL. WRIGHTON 3215.'

Whether Mr Taylor relies solely upon this method of advertisement for reciprocal female contacts or whether he employs other more productive devices, is open to conjecture, but whatever conclusion may be drawn he cannot be denied originality. Donald characteristically suggested that Mr Taylor might be a lovelorn, middle-aged bachelor with a passion either for mermaids or wild, beachcombing Hebridean maidens.

Donald had been employed specifically to look after the animals; a task to which he was admirably suited. The care of animals, particularly of tame wild animals is never as easy as is commonly supposed. To provide an animal with food is easy enough, but to feed an animal an intricately balanced diet of the right quantity and at correctly regulated intervals requires patience, skill and dedication. It was important too, that the animals knew and trusted their keeper; to win their trust and confidence meant long hours of patiently sitting and talking to them, feeding them by hand and gently handling them. It was still more important that Donald should know them; that he should be able to detect at a glance a misplaced feather or a bloodshot eye. Wild animals in captivity sicken quickly and suddenly if their conditions are wrong, and can be dead within hours of the first sign of discomfort. And so it was Donald's responsibility to attend to each of his charges in turn every morning and every night, a job which, even with our small collection, consumed a full third of the working day. Willie's task of the construction of pens and enclosures was also in capable hands and once I had marked out the site, provided the materials and explained the peculiarities of the beast his handiwork was to contain, it was certain that the work would be expeditiously fulfilled. Willie was a loyal and colourful character about whom I have much more to say in later chapters.

Our day, then, was divided between the construction of the enclosures, and the welfare of the animals. When the distractions were fewest, I myself slipped to Taichat to continue work on our book. Five years before, I had assisted David

Chaffe, the owner and director of the Westbury-upon-Trym Wildlife Park, with the construction and initial layout of his park, a similar scheme, but situated in entirely different, suburban surroundings on the outskirts of Bristol. David had found and purchased the twelve acre garden of a large private house. In its hey-day, it must have been in a delightful, rural village backwater, probably an hour's drive by chaise from Bristol. Those elegant days have long since given way to the city's industrial overflow, and the little village of Westbury has been enveloped on all sides to become just another *district*. The owners of the house fled before the flood, and its pilastered hall and large rooms are now partitioned to suit the needs of a home for the blind.

Yet, in David's Wildlife Park it is still possible to capture some of the tranquillity of an earlier era. The park is contained in a section of the Trym river valley, a section which at one time was skilfully and lovingly laid out by a landscape gardener. Many of the magnificent trees, weeping willows, wych elms and limes, the drooping birches, wild cherry, copper beech and various exotic conifers, are mature and provide welcome shade for the dappled fallow and minute Chinese water deer which now graze the sweet grass by the river.

The conception of a scheme like a Wildlife Park in such a densely populated area aroused much interest and publicity. While it was eventually beneficial, however, it was initially embarrassing. From the first day when a gang of men arrived with bundles of posts and coils of fencing wire, it was assumed that animals, wild and tame, great and small, were urgently wanted. Although at that time there was only one building capable of adequately housing an animal, they started to arrive in every shape and form : foxes, badgers, rabbits, birds with broken wings and legs – an astonishing variety from far and wide. The result was that valuable man-hours, which should have been profitably spent on the construction of permanent enclosures, were wasted on hurried, inadequate temporary quarters. I relate this pattern of events not in criticism of David Chaffe's administration – it would have been impossible on humanitarian grounds to say 'No, I'm sorry, we have no room,' to every child who appeared fervently clutching an injured bird in his arms – but as illustration of the circumstances I particularly wanted to avoid on Kyleakin Island.

The animals we already had on the island were, with the exception of Teko and the goats, temporarily quartered and it was my job to design and effect the construction of permanent pens for them as quickly as possible. We had not openly publicized our zoo, but our intentions were locally known and I feared a similar situation possibly exaggerated by the nature of our environment. The arrival of a few sick or oiled-up sea-birds and a stormwashed seal pup would have very considerably delayed our schedule.

My hours were divided between the drawing board and walking the island, measuring depth of peat, examining rock crevices to see which would provide shelter for what, and finally marking out the proposed sites with bamboo canes. But the atmosphere of the island was hardly conducive to concentration. There were gannets to watch, wheeling and diving, hurling themselves into the sea with the reckless dedication of Japanese suicide-pilots in the last war. There were rafts of eider ducks sometimes eighty or a hundred strong riding the gentle swell – patches of subtle-green and white as compact as a lily-leaf, the drakes cooing their muted, undulating love-song – and there were the little gritty bay-beaches with rows of tide-thrown weed and flotsam to turn over and explore. Sometimes I sat on the north headland with Max playing in the heather beside me, snapping at flies or tugging at the woody stems with superfluous puppy energy. There I watched the herring gulls and kittiwakes catching the eddying wind currents veering up the short cliff. Sometimes they zoomed up from below us so quickly that they were only a yard from my face as they skimmed over the headland; when they saw us they swerved away crying loudly in alarm, the air swishing through their primary feathers as they turned. Here I taught Max to rush barking at the gulls in order to frighten them away. Magnificent though they were, we could not afford to befriend them. Beneath their graceful exteriors were evil scavenging minds ever on the look-out for an easy meal. They learnt to wait until Donald had walked away after putting out Teko's fish; then down they came, swooping in to steal them before the old otter had trundled out of his den. Far worse, when the eider colony on the adjacent island was at the height of its breeding season the herring gulls, greater and lesser blackbacks, as well as local hoodies and ravens, flew in to steal the eggs and snatch the chicks from their nests and from the water. Later, when for another reason I wished to observe the gulls, I came to this headland and lay flat in the heather for long drowsy hours watching them pass, effortlessly, serenely on the wind.

Lunch was a token assembly on working days. Willie joined us with his piece – the Highland term for a lunch pack usually of sandwiches and oatcakes, while Donald and I drank coffee and nibbled at biscuits. Sometimes we listened to the lunchtime news on the radio, but with little attention; wars and demonstrations, strikes and discontentment; things not of our world but of another, infinitely distant, out of sight and out of reach. Occasionally there would be mention of Swansea or of the steel works at Port Talbot or of one of the vast oil refineries with which I had recently been so familiar, and I would find myself listening intently with momentarily renewed involvement. I could smell again the ammonia stench of the coke ovens and the acrid fumes of pickle-plants where the sheet steel is cleaned in baths of swirling acid, and I could hear again the hiss of escaping steam and the clunk of ponderous machinery; and faces, too, I could see; grey, lined faces of men I had known; and faces of men behind paper-littered desks, men pathetically awaiting promotion which had long since passed them by. But these moments were like scenes from a dream or from some dull play seen long ago; meaningless snatches of the past which only briefly obscured the sun till the light burst through again with fresh salt air, the murmur of the sea, and crying, wheeling gulls.

At some convenient point towards the end of the afternoon the working day ended and Donald took Willie back to Kyleakin village. The mail and newspapers seldom reached Skye before mid-afternoon, so this trip was a combined collection and shopping excursion and our daily contact with the local populace. It was possible to buy most household requisites in Kyleakin, but for the services of a chemist or an ironmonger we had to cross to Kyle on the ferry. The Kyleakin butcher provided us with meat for the dogs and our only other daily requirement for the animals was fish. Throughout the summer the Hebridean waters abound with mackerel and other less numerous species in local areas of favourable depth. It was necessary to keep the deep-freezes stocked since our daily consumption was already ten to twelve pounds of fish. The long evenings were ideally suited to fishing, an enjoyable operation often accompanied by a sunset so spectacular that the whole western horizon was afire with every shade of crimson and scarlet. When the sky was furrowed with wispy bands of altostratus cloud the colour ranged from the most delicate pearl-pinks to the deepest fiery red. Sometimes it was so breathtakingly beautiful that Donald and I rushed for our cameras to capture its ephemeral glory.

Those who have experienced the excitement of fishing a mackerel shoal with a single hook will appreciate the experience of using tackle known locally as a 'darrow' which supports six feathered hooks. It was possible to buy darrows with twenty hooks but we found these restrictive since they tangled too easily. Our technique required no skill or fishing knowledge at all; we simply rowed out into the Kyle with two darrows, a total of twelve hooks, trailing behind the dinghy. When we struck a shoal we stopped and hauled in our wildly jerking and twisting lines. Time after time we would pull them in, often with no pause at all. The hooks scarcely had time to sink out of sight before the line tugged at our fingers again, often with the combined force of six

fish and seldom less than four. On one memorable occasion
we rowed out to the light-buoy which was anchored in the
shipping channel three-quarters of a mile due west of the
lighthouse. It was a cloudy evening and as we arrived the
sun disappeared into a glowing velvet bank of high cumulus
cloud which obliterated Raasay from our view. The light
was rapidly fading, conditions ideally suited to our purpose,
and the sea around us reflected the deep olive sheen of old
claret bottles. We had really intended to fish for lythe, a big
silver fish of the cod family with a narrow jaw and menacing
eye, which frequented the sea-bed at this spot. We paid out
our darrows until the weights touched the bottom and the
lines slackened in our hands. Within ten minutes Donald
had caught four large lythe, each over a pound in weight,
and I had hauled in two 5 lb rock-cod on the same line, limp
soft-fleshed fish with barbels on their lower jaws giving them
a sinister, threatening glare. We unhooked them and threw
them into the bottom of the boat where they flipped and
gasped in their helpless predicament. Then, as we cast our
hooks overboard once more, the mackerel arrived. For the
next twenty minutes we hauled fish from the sea in multiples
of six. As fast as we unhooked and threw back our darrows
so they were snatched again from our grasp. Finally the
shoal was past and we sat there, our hands and arms smeared
to the elbow with fish slime, and our trousers sodden with
water from the lines we had hauled across our laps. The
bottom of the boat was a mass of quivering mackerel whose
staring eyes and gaping mouths detracted from the beauty
of their blue and green feathered backs. We fished on for a
few more minutes during which we each caught several more
rock-cod and lythe, and then we turned for home. The polythene basin we had with us to hold our catch was wholly
inadequate to cope with this quantity of fish, and when
we arrived back at the jetty it took us half an hour of constant ferrying to and from the house with two buckets apiece
before the dinghy was empty. When the load was finally
sorted and weighed we discovered to our amazement that an

hour's fishing had yielded the sum of 184 fish, 157 of which were mackerel, 11 rock-cod and 16 lythe. A total weight of 214 lbs 10 ozs.

This story has a sequel which belies any claim to skill or special fishing techniques on our part. As the autumn drew on so the mackerel migrated to distant waters and our success, never again as dramatic as that evening's haul, waned with the season. By mid-October our deep frozen fish stocks were seriously depleted and we fished the quickly darkening evenings with a new urgency. The mackerel, it seemed, had almost completely gone and the result of two hours' fishing up and down the Kyle was all too often a pitiful single fish, usually a coal-fish or lythe. Our only regular visitor to the island was the lighthouse keeper Simon MacLean, who lived in Kyleakin and was responsible for the maintenance of our lighthouse and a similar light at Kyle Rhea which lay five miles round the north-eastern point of Skye at the entrance of the Sound of Sleat. Simon was in the habit of rowing across to the island on fine evenings to fulfil his duty. As he rowed he trailed a six-hook darrow exactly similar to our own tackle. We therefore found it a little irritating when, only an hour after Donald and I had returned from a lengthy fishing expedition which had taken us far out into the Sound of Raasay in one direction and far down into Loch Alsh in the other and had yielded a paltry handful of small fish, Simon arrived at the island jetty with between thirty and forty fish flapping in the bottom of his boat. On many occasions we watched him gaily pulling in his laden darrow as he drifted gently across to the island when sometimes, only minutes before, our own efforts had proved fruitless in precisely the same spot. The answer could only lie in our complete lack of experience and feel. Simon examined our tackle, even lent us his own darrow and his boat, but to no avail. Clearly we had no mastery of the art, and no matter how intent our concentration or how endless our patience, we continued to catch no fish. The solution to our problem, however, was close at hand. With characteristic generosity Simon offered to fish for us whenever he crossed to the island, and we happily surrendered this part of our duty to such an obvious master.

Since my arrival on Kyleakin Island the weather had been fine and warm. Willie had made good progress with the bird of prey aviaries behind the house, and I had reached a point in the planning of the zoo where I could proceed no further without direct consultation with Gavin. And so, leaving the island in Donald's capable hands, I took the ferry on 28 August to Kyle of Lochalsh and drove east through the early morning mist to Inverness.

FIVE

Hospital

I entered the hospital quietly and made my way on tip-toe down the long, empty corridors to Gavin's room. He was in a small private ward and I had to inquire from a porter as to its exact location. I tapped gently on the door in case he was asleep and was a little startled when a cheery voice sang out 'Entrez'. As I pushed open the door, a haze of blue cigarette smoke swirled out to greet me.

Gavin was reclining on a mound of pillows wearing a bright red polo-necked pullover and browsing through a small volume of Roy Campbell's poems. Roy Campbell was a friend with whom Gavin had often corresponded, and that book of poems and Kathleen Raine's *The Hollow Hill* were two books which he particularly prized and kept in gilt-decorated morocco leather jackets on his desk at Kyleakin, and now beside his hospital bed. Poetry was of great importance to Gavin. He modestly described himself as 'a half-poet with a hyper-sensitive temperament'. Half-poet or not, his own verses had not infrequently appeared in well known weeklies and in the pages of his autobiographical books.

In March that year when I had visited Kyleakin Island for the first time we had often sat up till late into the night, and invariably the conversation had turned to poetry. We had picked out our favourite verses from the extensive library at Kyleakin and read them aloud to the accompaniment of the crackling drift-wood fire and the rhythmical breathing of the dogs at our feet. I remember starting timidly with childhood favourites like Brooke's *Clouds*, and Masefield's *Beauty* and *Up on the Downs*. Gavin chose verses from W. H. Auden and, spurred by my chidhood recollections, quoted whole sections of James Thomson's *The City of Dreadful Night*, faultlessly and with his eyes closed as if he were reading direct from a mental page.

On another night he read some of the lilting biblical prose of Oscar Wilde's short stories : *The Selfish Giant* and *The Young King*. Later still we dabbled in twentieth century poems by Ken Geering and other *Breakthru* contributors, but we made little headway. Gavin confessed to a blind-spot for much contemporary verse and inevitably we reverted to works we knew and understood. Now, it seemed that it was with his friends' verses that he chose to while away the long hospital hours.

He slapped the book shut and placed it on the table beside the bed.

'Come on in,' he said with a grin. 'Sorry about the smoke. I suppose we'd better open a window.'

I struggled with the window and by opening the top half and holding the door open for a few moments we managed to disperse most of the smoke into the corridor. Gavin tugged at his beard. 'If the man in the next ward hasn't got lung cancer already, he'll get it now,' he laughed. That turned out to be the cruellest piece of dramatic irony I have heard.

Gavin was a compulsive cigarette smoker; at one period he smoked up to eighty cigarettes a day – an excess he publicized with masochistic pride. Kyleakin Island was the only household I have ever known which could boast of a box of cigarettes beside the lavatory *and* the bath. There were in fact boxes of cigarettes and ash-trays beside every bed in the house and within reach of every chair, sofa or stool. Several years before, when I first visited his famous house at Sandaig, I remember emptying the ash-trays in Gavin's study at the end of the house. Their contents, the discarded residue of two days' smoking, half-filled a medium sized waste-paper basket.

He had dismissed lung-cancer as the cause of his ill-health. He had, in fact, been cleared of the suspicion of it in 1967, as he described in his last book, *Raven Seek Thy Brother*. Subsequent check-ups had also proved negative. I accepted his own conviction at that stage without question. I knew he had had an extraordinary medical history throughout his life, starting at the age of sixteen with a rare blood condition from which he nearly died, *Purpura Haemorrhagica* – an illness which privileged him with a memorable visit from Lord Horder, the King's physician.

More recently he had contracted an alarming variety of rare diseases indigenous to the many unwholesome quarters of the world in which he had travelled. Internal injury and ulceration were also on the list, and it was this last which he suspected to be the cause of his present discomfort.

At the best of times he was a difficult patient. In hospital he liked to entertain his friends as generously and lavishly as he did at home; and the necessary accoutrements, a table crowded with bottles and glasses and endless packets of cigarettes for his own continuous consumption as well as his visitors', were conspicuous additions to the room's austere equipment. On one occasion some years before, he had become quite seriously ill at Sandaig. The local doctor, a close friend and confidant, walked the long, winding path down the hill in appalling weather conditions to see him. Gravely he advised Gavin to leave Sandaig – which could hardly be described as the most accessible or suitable house for medical treatment – and to go into hospital in Inverness as soon as possible. It took many hours of persuasion before Gavin agreed to accept this obviously sensible advice.

'Oh, but I've got some friends coming on Thursday,' he argued, 'and so-and-so is coming to stay for a week from next Saturday, so I can't go until he's gone. And then I'm off to North Africa on Tuesday week, and I can't delay that. Oh, and there's a company meeting in London the day before my flight and that can't possibly be cancelled. I really don't see how I'm going to fit this hospital visit in.' And so on until the doctor was biting his lip in exasperation.

Now, as I poured myself a drink and pulled a chair up to

his bedside, I could see that the hospital staff were not having an easy time.

'How do you get away with this?' I asked, waving my hand at the array of bottles and cigarettes.

'They've given up protesting,' he replied with an angelic look. A look which is in fact not at all easily described because, following an attack of acute conjunctivitis in the Sahara whilst working on his book *Lords of the Atlas*, Gavin habitually wore dark glasses so that the expression in his eyes, which was often far from angelic, was invariably concealed. Yet he contrived, by raising his eyebrows above the rim of his glasses, and by placidly stroking and curling the end of his Saudi Arabian styled beard, to look angelic. His beards, which were periodically removed and re-grown, were subjects of perpetual attention. In and around them he built many mannerisms, and it was often possible to detect his mood and even his train of thought from the way he stroked, pulled at or curled their pointed ends. He was a man of impeccable grooming and he kept his beards perfectly trimmed, never a whisker out of place. His hands, too, were to me a source of envy and admiration. He had small neat hands, almost white with cleanliness; often out of place, I thought, in the midst of boats and ropes, out-board engines and gunnels sticky with fish-slime, when everyone else's were suitably soiled. But it was his beards which occupied the greatest attention, and the photograph reproduced on the back cover of the first edition of *Ring of Bright Water*, in which he wears an earlier, more rounded beard, was one of his favourites. Sometimes when friends were trying to date accurately events in his life he would ask, 'Was I bearded then, or not?' as if he maintained some tabulated mental chronology marked off in bearded and unbearded eras.

We talked briefly about his illness, but it was of secondary importance to his enthusiasm for the progression of the zoo. For an hour he fired questions at me about the work we had done. He busily drew little sketches to illustrate details of wiring and fencing the animal enclosures, and continued to doodle with them long after the subject was dropped. By the time I left several sheets were covered with little vignettes of animals peering comically over fences, caricatures of birds of prey – great vulturine hawks and eagles, incongruously perched on posts, wickedly eyeing some little furry beast in a neighbouring cage. Drawings made alive and real with the confidence of a skilled cartoonist.

Among his other talents Gavin had an enviable flair for visual art. He was skilled with brush and pencil and for some years after the failure of his Hebridean shark fishery on the island of Soay in 1949, he had been a professional portrait painter. Above the sink in the scullery at Kyleakin hung a large gilt-framed portrait of a very aristocratic looking lady. One day I asked for its story. He told me that he had worked for some weeks on the canvas, living in great comfort in the subject's country home, and that both he and the lady were well pleased with it. One morning, however, as the portrait neared completion, Gavin was summoned to the library. There the noble lord explained that he was, that morning, divorcing his wife and since it was she who had commissioned the painting, and since she now had no money, it was unlikely that he would ever be paid his fee. So Gavin departed with the portrait under his arm and it was later relegated to the Kyleakin scullery.

There were other canvases of his about the house at Kyleakin. Some of Sandaig : quick, impressionist seascapes in oils with that superb mountain back-cloth; and others, portraits of friends or those members of the household who were most commonly about him. There was a self-portrait, too, a painting of a handsome young man, unbearded and with a carefree look about him, dressed in the type of thick-knit sweater he commonly wore. The portrait was again unfinished, unsigned and undated, modestly hung in an outbuilding, and hanging askew from a nail banged hurriedly into the white-washed wall. That painting was not clear or concise in detail, and close inspection revealed blotchy, dabbed brush-strokes which appeared to confuse the outline of his face and defy expression. But later, as I worked in the store-room, and became more closely acquainted with the portrait I became aware of a deeper quality within the brush-work which, from a distance, revealed form and presence so that I sometimes sensed the watching eyes and looked up from what I was doing to meet their stare. Yes, perhaps *life* is the right word. One day I stood on a fish box and straightened the picture on its nail.

At noon I left the hospital to go and have lunch in town and in the early afternoon I met up with Richard Frere who was at that time managing director of Gavin's private company, Gavin Maxwell Enterprises, Ltd, and together we returned to the hospital. Gavin had seen his doctor in the intervening time and had made some provisional arrangements for his return to the island. He was to undergo an immediate course of treatment and then, provided that he felt fit enough, he would be able to leave hospital to return at a later date for more treatment dependent upon his reaction to the first application. He was still convinced of his absolute recovery.

He greeted us warmly with this news and immediately plunged into detailed plans and preparations for his dismissal. If a later return to hospital was to be necessary he was anxious to do as much as he could in the meantime. He had made arrangements with the owner of the island of Pabay, a low, dune-like island six miles west of Kyleakin Island, to shoot rabbits from an excessive wild stock resident there, so that we would have a good deep-freeze supply of meat for the carnivorous animals in our collection. Gavin was a remarkable shot with both rifle and shotgun and he was keen to be present on any expedition we might make there.

I am often asked how it is possible for a man to be an ardent lover of animals and an accomplished naturalist and, at the same time, like Gavin Maxwell, to be an avid sportsman – the very essence of which involves killing those animals he professes to love. It is perhaps significant that the lives of many great naturalists of the present day and the past have often gone through prolonged periods of persecution of one form of game or another. It was certainly a conflict that Gavin was acutely aware of and in his first book, *Harpoon at a Venture*, about his island of Soay shark fishery (which itself involved the commercial killing of basking sharks), he goes to some lengths to reconcile these two apparently conflicting interests. In his examination of cruelty he concludes that men live by instilled standards of conduct, condoning those cruelties which the code of their upbringing allows and condemning those that are exactly similar but outside the sphere of their personal experience. Men reared in a sporting tradition are early conditioned to accept death as part of the course of everyday life, while those sheltered from it are blind to its continual occurrence and are shocked by others' apparent insensitivity to it. But beyond this difference in outlook, Gavin spoke often of the hunter's appreciation of his quarry. Brought up in a similar sporting vein, I am conscious of the validity of that belief. The shot who has no interest in the birds and beasts he shoots is not a sportsman. It is certainly true that the men who know most about fish are anglers and those who are most knowledgeable on gamebirds are usually those who shoot them. And I am conscious too of a genuine value in stalking a beast in its natural context, that of predator and prey, as opposed to simply stalking to observe it. The real appreciation of the senses; scent, sight and hearing; the subtleties of light and shade in camouflage and the understanding of speed and movement are only really learnt in the struggle against wind and contour, only truly manifest in the hunter's racing pulse.

Gavin believed that through his sporting youth he had achieved an intimacy with those wild species he persecuted which led him to a fuller and richer appreciation of all animal life. No sportsman ever likes to wound a beast, a clean kill being the ultimate perfection of all shooting, and Gavin's considerable skill with rifle and shotgun was a tribute to real sportsmanship. I had watched him sniping with a .22 rifle at hoodie crows and greater black-backed gulls which made regular marauding raids on the eider chicks breeding on the little island adjacent to Kyleakin Island, and I marvelled at his accuracy. The corpses I recovered had all been instantly killed by a single bullet through the head.

From whole school holidays dedicated to the persecution of rabbits in Somerset before the myxomatosis epidemic, I knew exactly what difficult targets rabbits could be and I viewed the projected expedition to Pabay with enthusiasm. I had never actually shot with Gavin, and while I knew my own ability to be vastly inferior to his, I was anxious to prove my worth.

Whilst we were talking about Pabay and our proposed expedition there I was reminded of an incident which had occurred a few days earlier on Kyleakin Island, and I took the opportunity of asking Gavin about it.

One evening I had walked down to the lighthouse to watch the sunset from the advantage of its seventy-foot summit. I had climbed the tiny spiral stair and the iron ladders which connected the three levels of the tower, up its tall cylindrical interior to the lamp-room at the top. The lamp-room was small and round with walls some seven feet high made entirely of thick plate glass. A small doorway led out on to a steel parapet around the outside for maintenance and cleaning, and the whole was capped by a copper dome and a weathercock which creaked eerily from above. The light itself was a white light; a gas flame served by pressurized bottles on the ground floor and magnified to the required intensity by huge glass prisms mounted around it. Standing beside the light and looking up and down the narrow seaway between the island and the rocks of Skye directly opposite, one viewed the passage through large, clear-glass panels. But between the two clear panels, which ran round the larger part of the circumference of the room, the glass was tinted red to signify danger to any vessel approaching from the wrong direction

The effect of standing beside the clear glass panels was

quite frightening; the transparency of the glass was so complete that one felt uncomfortably exposed to the sheer drop and the foam of the waves breaking over the rocks seventy feet below. But to look out through the adjacent red panel was conversely reassuring : the white of the breakers mellowed to an unrealistic pink, and the whole magnificent seascape and its rugged backcloth glowed in varying shades of red as though in some incredible, all-pervasive sunset. The analogy with the metaphorical rose-tinted spectacles was too good to miss, and later became a standing joke between Donald and myself.

It was while I was enjoying the novelty of this discovery for the first time that I noticed a disturbance in the surface of the sea several hundred yards out in the wide expanse to the west of the island. I moved quickly to a clear panel and focused my binoculars on the spot. For a chilling moment I saw a sharp, sabre-like fin cut the surface of the water and disappear. I had never seen a killer-whale, but I knew very well that only one beast in British coastal waters possessed a fin as vertical and menacing as that. I peered intently at the place it had disappeared and again, far beyond, thankfully heading away from the island, I saw the blade of its fin slice through the waves, its apex rising out of the water so that the black dome of its back and the contrasting white of its flank showed clearly above the surface. I watched for some minutes after that but the light was rapidly failing and I did not see it again.

I knew that Gavin had made a study of whales and dolphins during his shark-fishery days, and I lost no time in relating this experience to him. His face suddenly grew stern. 'Have you seen it since then?' he asked gravely.

'No,' I replied, 'I have searched the sea most days for any activity but I've seen nothing but basking sharks.'

'Thank God for that,' he said, clearly relieved.

'Why?' I asked.

'Because as long as there are killers about the island waters we shall see no seals, no porpoises and dolphins, no otters,

and precious little else. Killers are exactly what their name
implies and in a killing mood a party of killer-whales will
devastate a whole seal colony and frighten everything else
from the area.'

At once I saw the reason for his concern. The very essence
of the island's charm lay in its sea-birds and the frequent
visits from seals and porpoises. If a killer chose to habituate
our island waters for the summer, our most valuable natural
assets would certainly disappear.

'What do we do if it comes back?' I asked.

'We do our utmost to shoot it with a high-powered rifle,'
Gavin replied, '–from *land*,' he added with emphasis. 'In
fact,' he continued, 'if a killer-whale does decide to frequent
our area – and in my absence I rely upon you to look out
for it every day – then I expressly forbid any employee of the
company to stray further than half a mile from the island or
mainland in our dinghy. There are some very unpleasant
stories about killers attacking small boats and it is a risk I
cannot allow to be taken.' We sat in thoughtful silence, then
Gavin asked, 'What calibre is your rifle?'

'.270,' I replied.

'Has it got a telescopic sight?'

'Yes.'

'Good. Keep it handy, and if you see the beast again, get
as close as you can on land, wait till it rises and aim just in
front of its eye. If you're smart you should be able to get two
bullets into it before it submerges.'

I swallowed hard and said I would do my best. Thankfully
the occasion never arose. Seals continued to frequent the
island waters and porpoises and dolphins regularly passed us
curving through the water as gracefully as the gulls glided
overhead; but Gavin's stern face, accentuated by his dark
glasses, and the slow, precise enunciation of his warning
ran deep, and in the months which followed I spent many
hours up on the headlands scanning the sea to our north
and west for a glimpse of that thin black sabre.

*   *   *

At four o'clock a nurse arrived with a tea-trolley and we joined Gavin in his afternoon meal. I noticed that he ate very little, remarking casually that he was not hungry and I thought it symptomatic of ulceration. But he was still very talkative and he inquired closely into the well-being of old Teko, the otter. Teko was one of Gavin's last tangible associations with Sandaig and the idyllic years of *Ring of Bright Water*, and, like any pet which had bridged years of great happiness and great sorrow, Teko was very dear to him. He was conscious, too, that Teko was bound to be unhappy during his absence from the island and we discussed every detail of Teko's daily routine; his food, the water in his pool, the central-heating in his den and the amount of time Donald spent with him every day. While it was important that Teko should have regular daily contact with humans, it was a delicate affair since he was known to be ill-tempered at times and Gavin was most anxious to avoid a repetition of the awful accident with Terry Nutkins' fingers when he was savaged by Edal, the otter which died in the Sandaig fire. Happily, Donald and Teko seemed to have taken well to each other and Donald was able to handle the old otter without any sign of aggression or jealousy. Gavin seemed reassured.

A little later the floor sister came in and said that the doctor would be soon visiting Gavin and they wanted to clear up the room and make his bed. Richard and I took the hint and prepared to leave. Gavin shook us warmly by the hand saying that the next time I saw him would be on the island. It was a cheering thought to depart with, and as I drove west into the glare of the sinking sun I could think of no obstacle which might prevent the continuation of the island zoo or hinder the progress of our book.

SIX

Portrait of a Henchman

The day after I arrived to live on the island I met Willie MacAskill for the second time. Our first meeting had been in March when I was a guest in the house, and although I had been introduced to him he had hurried off to work on a stock fence he was erecting at the north end of the island. During the rest of my stay I had seen him only fleetingly, a swarthy figure who spoke little and anyway seemed far too busy to talk. Our second meeting was of a different nature. I sat at the desk in the long-room in front of the big window with the telescope trained on to the dinghy which was creeping sluggishly through the seven-knot tidal race between the island and Kyleakin beach. It was a fresh morning and the bows of the boat chopped into the angry little waves which pounced diagonally at her hull and broke away again with curling white crests. Donald had surrendered the outboard to a more experienced hand, and was sitting for'ard with the collar of his jacket up around his ears and his back into the breeze. At last the dinghy broke free of the clutching tide and lurched forward into smoother water. I saw Donald turn as Willie pointed ahead of the boat : two black guillemots rose from the water almost beneath the bows and scrambled away to the left with a flurry of black and white wings and little orange feet paddling frantically at the surface in their haste to rise into flight. I swung the telescope after them; a hundred yards of rapid wing beats and they glided like partridges to settle on the water again, their feet stuck out in front of them to land. They shuffled their wings, wagged their stumpy tails, and bobbed and dipped on the swell. When I returned the glass to the dinghy it had disappeared. They had rounded the rocks beyond the jetty and entered the cove to land out of sight of the house. I whistled to Max to follow, left the house and walked down the path to meet them.

I had been warned that I might have difficulty in understanding Willie. He was a Gaelic-speaking outer Isleman from Tarbert on Harris, and he spoke English with a thick Hebridean brogue. That, however, was the least of the problem. Willie had no teeth. Now that I have become accustomed to this I find it hard to imagine Willie with even a fraction of the normal complement of teeth, and harder still to imagine his speech punctuated by the rolling Scottish 'r' and the glottal aspirate. He was happily content in the belief that by undaunted repetition someone sooner or later would get the gist of what he was saying. Vowels alone were the milestones by which one might conjecture this, but I was completely unprepared for the unintelligible flow of words with which he greeted my approach.

'Hullo hir! Hirrithoohir? Howaryoohir hin I hawooyhaw?' He bellowed, displaying his bare gums in a broad, friendly smile.

('Hullo Sir! Is it you Sir? How are ye Sir since I saw you before?')

To continue to record our dialogue phonetically would be to test the reader's patience too far. At the risk of failing to convey my difficulty in understanding him, I shall therefore translate.

I made some remark about the weather and pushed forward a welcoming hand. Willie shook it heartily and rambled on in the same undulating, benevolent style. To me it was all completely meaningless. There was barely a word I could understand.

'Hey!' I said. 'Hold on, hold on.'

Willie looked momentarily hurt.

'You must speak very slowly and carefully so that I can get used to your Highland accent.'

He beamed again and started off on another burst of

volubility. I gave up and walked him back to the house.

Somehow I had to find out what work he was currently engaged on and a host of other details about the construction of the zoo. Slowly and laboriously we pieced together the outline of his duties on the island, and a routine of work for the coming weeks. Now, a year later I can converse reasonably fluently with Willie, but it has not come about through any recognition of his words; there is no English parallel to a large proportion of them, and many still remain a complete mystery to me; I suspect that some are Gaelic Anglicizations and vice versa, words which without an intimate knowledge of his native tongue in its dialect I shall never be able to decipher. But I have learned, through gesticulation and mime and trial and error, to understand most of what he says.

Fundamentally Willie was a seaman. His merchant service record reveals a score of honourable discharges and credits for ability and general conduct covering a span of eighteen years, but besides this exemplary record he had turned his hand during forty-five years of active working life to a wide variety of occupations : crofting, shepherding, working in a sawmill, operating a tunnelling machine on civil engineering projects, standing civilian guard over ammunition boats during the war, and gillie to stalkers of the Highland deer. There were few fields in which Willie had not had some experience, and as a handyman on the island he was superb. He had also, during his merchant service, been, I understood, a henchman. This was a mercantile designation I had not met before.

'Whose henchman?' I inquired.

'Henchman to the big boat,' came the surprised reply. (Which in fact sounded like 'Hanchmun toother hib boot'.)

I was intrigued and sought further information. 'How many Henchmen were there aboard your vessel?'

'Six,' came the unmistakable reply confirmed by as many fingers. No wiser but none the less determined to find out about Merchant Navy henchmen, I pressed Willie no further in case my search led me deeper into the linguistic wilderness. My inquiries led nowhere. A retired merchant sailor of approximately the same vintage as Willie whom I met in Inverness dolefully shook his head. Never in all his thirty years of sailing the seas had he come across a henchman. 'The man's invented it,' was his only solution. I was disinclined to agree. There had been an air of importance about the way Willie first replied to my question. 'A henchman, Sir,' he had answered curtly and proudly, without hesitation and with a slight, scarcely noticeable straightening of the back and shoulders. No, it was not an invention; whatever a henchman might have been, Willie had been it. I took to the dictionary. I tried benchman, tenchman, trenchman and many others but the nearest I found was wenchman which, although it strongly connotes sailors and dockland was hardly suitable and existed only in a dictionary of slang.

Weeks passed until one stormy October day we discovered our stocks of diesel fuel to be dangerously low, and I decided that we must brave the seas and make a trip to Kyle with two forty-gallon drums. Donald could not swim and had had little experience of boats in rough weather so I decided to accompany Willie myself. Gingerly we manoeuvred the *Amara*, the island launch, in to the jetty and loaded the empty drums aboard her heaving stern. Willie threw the launch into reverse and, as we churned away from the island, I lashed the drums securely into position behind the centrally mounted engine. As we broke away from the lee of the island we surged and dipped before the wind while the waves loomed fiercely up behind us, pitching us forward and dragging at the stout clinker-built hull as they sped past. Willie stood unperturbedly at the wheel, the wind lashing his back and the spray running in rivulets down the grooves of his leathery face.

We battled valiantly down the mile of open seaway to Kyle, but, as we neared the pier, and I saw the size of the waves smashing into its rigid concrete sides, I shouted to Willie to heave to and wait for the wind to drop. Hebridean storms are often short lived and I thought that an hour might see it through. Whether Willie heard me or not I shall never know. His muffled reply was snatched from his lips by the wind and hurled away. This was his element and as far as I could see he was loving it. We ploughed on past the pier still twenty yards out from its threatening wall. Then, as the stern drew level with its windward side, I saw Willie glance back over his shoulder, gauge the wind and the distance and pull the wheel hard to starboard with all the assurance of twenty years at sea. The launch heaved as he opened the throttle, hung momentarily across the wind and bit stubbornly into the racing waves. Slowly and ponderously we came about until, triumphantly, we were round through 180° and dead level with the end of the pier. I clung silently to the drums in the stern well and watched with admiration. Willie was master and I was humbly thankful to be his subordinate. At that moment his words came echoing back to me : 'A henchman, Sir,' he had said. Suddenly the truth dawned. A launchman he was, certainly and unequivocally, and I laughed as the *Amara* lurched again, turned and crept into calmer water as we drew evenly and surely under Willie's masterful guidance along the sheltered side of the pier.

Willie lived at Ardminish, a small coastal settlement of tiny crofts and but-and-bens which lay five miles west of Kyle-akin on the North Skye coast. He owned a smart white-washed croft with a bright red door and six acres of poor pasture on which he grew hay and potatoes and grazed a cow and a dozen hens. The land was flat and rough, broken only by dykes and fences, and the wee house faced the rising sun and bared its shoulders to the prevailing wind which swept in across Skye from the Atlantic and rattled the door and moaned in the chimney. Fifty yards below the house the grass ended abruptly and gave way to tidal mud where flourished the marsh samphire and the creeping eel-grass. Beyond, low and dune-like, three miles out lay the island of

Gavin Maxwell *c.* 1968

Kyleakin Lighthouse and the Cuillin Hills of Skye

Kyleakin Lighthouse and Island from Kyleakin beach on Skye

The island house facing east down Loch Alsh

The 'long room' in the island house showing the Michael Ayrton wax and bone Icarus on the end wall

Gavin Maxwell stands in the doorway of the gutted ruin of 'Camusfeàrna'

Gavin Maxwell outside the island house. The ×40 telescope was always at hand

From left to right: Gavin Maxwell, Jimmy Watt, Richard Frere and Willie MacAskill

Breakfast outside. *From left to right:* Jimmy Watt, Peugeot, Max, Donald Mitchell and the author

Our gannet in juvenile plumage

Richard Frere and Owl

Donald Mitchell at the wheel of the *Amara* in a Force 8 gale

Gavin Maxwell and Teko

Teko, Andrew Scot and Gavin Maxwell

Pabay; an island of pasture and marshes like a mottled lily-leaf on an enormous pond; and beyond again, dim with the horizon, the rocky shapes of the Crowlin Isles and the Applecross peninsula.

In the mornings Willie set out on his bicycle to pedal the five winding miles to Kyleakin to meet the dinghy on the beach. I am told that the bicycle had at one time been motor assisted, but whenever I saw it it was conspicuously a push-bike and usually more push than pedal. In the evenings his tactics were a little more subtle. When Donald delivered him safely to Kyleakin beach he adjourned directly to the local hotel bar which was conveniently placed at the top of the beach. Here, he awaited the arrival of any likely itinerant with a car, and, for the price of a dram, he secured a lift home. Not always, however, had his hospitality such sinister motivation.

One bright September evening I crossed with Willie and Donald to Kyleakin. My car, for which I had had little use that summer, required periodic attention and since it was a fine evening I offered to run Willie home and call in at the garage on the way back. My car (called for some illogical reason, Burgess) was an old lady of great character and distinction. She was big and black and ponderous, but her capacious engine, when suitably encouraged, was capable of a remarkable turn of speed. At that time, during the course of fifteen years' life and an honourable total of a hundred and thirty-four thousand miles, she had consumed an estimated seven thousand gallons of petrol. Willie sank back into the welcoming embrace of her old leather seats and we swept sedately up the road leaving a column of thick white dust swirling in our wake.

When we reached the croft its white walls glared in the burning sun and the sea beyond lay mirror-calm around its islands; Scalpay and Raasay faint and dusty grey in the haze, and Pabay vivid and luxuriant in a shimmering liquid desert. The bright red door stood ajar and a fat hen dozed outside on the step.

'You're coming in, Sir?' Willie asked insistently. West Highland hospitality is forceful and genuine.

'Thank you Willie, I will, but only for a few minutes. I have to meet Donald back at the boat before long.' My hesitation was disregarded. Willie strode to the open door and bellowed to his wife; the hen, wary of its owner's boots, scuttled off down the path clucking in distress. I was ushered through the bright red door and into the hall. It was tiny and dark and the air was chill after the sticky heat outside. The room to the right of the hall was the living-room; a small square box with a low white ceiling yellowing with age, sparsely furnished with two chairs before a tiled grate, which, to my astonishment held a small fire of glowing coals on what was probably the hottest day of the summer. Against the wall behind the chairs stood a small folding table with three plain dining-room chairs tucked neatly beneath its sides. Behind these, against the far wall of the room, was a gigantic mahogany dresser. It dominated the entire room like a huge Yorkshire washer-woman, feet astride and arms akimbo, occupying a full quarter of the floor space and reaching up to within a few inches of the ceiling. It was an overpowering Victorian intrusion into a world of fresh, timeless simplicity. And yet, for all its corpulence, it fulfilled the combined functions of many lesser and more elegant pieces. The best china occupied the reaches of its upper shelves and a more utilitarian assortment, amid a jumble of brightly coloured cake and biscuit tins, tea caddies and other paraphernalia, existed below. Its drawers contained bed and table linen, cutlery, sewing equipment, brown paper and string, pots of paint, brushes, jars of screws, staples, nails, nuts and bolts, and, appropriately, from beneath a jumble of assorted tools and other mechanical oddments, there protruded the tell-tale coloured corner of a long discarded income-tax form. Below the drawers, the closed doors of dark and cavernous cupboards concealed stores of home made preserves, superfluous pots and pans, boots and shoes, imperishable household provisions and cut peats for the fire.

Sara MacAskill emerged from the tiny kitchen which adjoined the living-room and came forward to meet me. She was a quiet, retiring woman with an ageless wrinkled face and penetrating sea-blue eyes, and her fine grey hair was gathered in a haphazard knot at the back of her head. She was dressed plainly in a long grey tunic dress, thick woven hose and blunt, buttoned shoes. Around her waist she wore an apron on which she continually wiped her tired, frail hands. She spoke in a strong, lilting, almost Teutonic accent and no sooner had she withdrawn her greeting hand from mine than Willie bellowed at her in their native tongue and she hurried away to execute his command.

'Will ye see ma dogs, Sir?' Willie asked without any intention of letting me refuse.

I followed him out into the brilliant sunlight and round the croft to a corrugated iron lean-to byre on the south side. The field immediately in front of the house was dotted with freshly turned mounds of yellow hay. Willie unfastened the knotted string on the byre door to a crescendo of frenzied barking from within. He still did part-time shepherding on Skye and his two collies were, as he put it, more important than the boots on his feet in a land of vast unfenced slopes and rugged corries. The dogs pranced wildly round us thrusting their pointed black and white faces up at us with obvious pleasure. There was a terrier too; a scruffy little brown dog resembling a Yorkshire but of stockier build and shorter leg, with a tail which might have been borrowed from a poodle; it wagged not from the base of the dog's spine but from its neck, a curious wiggling action like that of an eel. This was the house dog and for that purpose it was admirably suited. It produced a volume of sound utterly disproportionate to its diminutive frame and of the pitch and jangling quality of a cheap alarm clock.

'No better dogs a man could wish for,' mumbled Willie as he ordered them back into the dark shed.

As we returned to the house I glanced obviously at my watch and suggested that it was time I returned to Kyleakin. But it was a wasted gesture. Highland hospitality relies upon an utter disregard for time, and to these folk it was a foregone conclusion that I would share their evening meal. When we re-entered the living-room I was astonished to find the table set and a pot of tea steaming beside the fire.

Boiled mutton and potatoes are simple fare but the simplicity and sincerity of the meal, to the extent of self-sacrifice — for the food apportioned to me amounted to twice that on either of the MacAskill plates — gave it the savour and *delicatesse* of the finest continental cuisine. And there were freshly baked scones dripping with salty butter and strong, sweet tea which was strangely more refreshing on that hot evening than the longest iced drink would have been. I departed, finally, when the sun had gone from the sky and only a fading light beyond the peaks on the horizon revealed the position of its going down. The land was cooling and a warm breeze had begun to creep in from the sea; with it came the liquid, bubbling call of curlews as they planed in to pitch below the house on mud left bare by the ebbing tide. I stood for a moment outside the bright red door and considered a remark Willie had made earlier in the evening when he had proudly shown me, with a sweep of his arm, the extent of his estate : 'I've got everything here, Sir, in these six acres that a man could wish for, except money, and I've no use for that.'

On the evening of my return from visiting Gavin in hospital in Inverness I met Willie on Kyleakin beach. 'How's the Major, Sir?' he asked with concern on his old swarthy face. (Gavin's wartime rank persisted where he was well known on the west coast although he never used it himself.)

'I'm afraid he's not better yet Willie,' I replied, 'but he hopes to be back soon.'

'What ails him, Sir?'

'It seems to be an old tummy trouble which is playing

him up again Willie, but we're not very sure.' Willie said goodnight and wandered off towards the hotel bar mumbling something about not trusting doctors with a constipated donkey. I had met that attitude before in the Highlands and I chuckled as I sat down on the shingle beach to await the arrival of the dinghy.

From the beach the island was clearly in view. I could see Donald leave the house and walk down the path to the jetty, the old deer-hounds, Hazel and Dirk, nimbly picking their way over the ground at his heels and Max, ebullient as ever, prancing wildly around them. A second later I heard the sound of his vigorous playful bark echoing across the half-mile of seaway between us. Max had not been a mistake. The island was an ideal place to bring up a dog and he was quickly growing into a fine, well proportioned labrador with the friendly nature characteristic of his breed. I had been a little apprehensive of the reception the deer-hounds would give such a young dog when we first arrived on the island. I had imagined that they might have resented such an intrusion into their otherwise unchallenged territory, but my fears were ill-founded. Donald and I had introduced the dogs carefully and quietly, a firm hold on them all. That introduction was the non-event of the week. Dirk and Hazel showed no more interest in Max than a cow shows in a rabbit. They sniffed vaguely in his direction, then ambled off about their business. Max, on the other hand displayed immediate interest, and although his first approaches were cautious and restrained, the temptation to play quickly undermined his fear and within minutes of their acquaintance he was dancing happily around them. During the months which followed I often had cause to marvel at the equanimity of those old deer-hounds. Day after day Max tried every aggravating and exasperating puppyhood mischief to persuade the old dogs to play with him – but completely without success. He pranced round them in circles, darting swiftly between their lank, slender legs; he barked at them when they were eating, sleeping and lazing idly in the sun; he chewed their tails and he tugged at their shaggy ears. Sometimes, after prolonged provocation when I feared that their patience must surely break, I rebuked Max strongly and called him away to leave the old hounds in peace. But sooner or later he would creep back when my attention was averted. They never did turn on him nor did they ever play with him, but there arose out of this relationship a trust so entire that it can only be compared with that of parent and offspring. On dark autumn evenings when the shutters rattled and the wind moaned round the house and in the chimney, Donald and I would build a roaring driftwood fire in the long-room and the dogs would edge in as close to the grate as they dared and stretch themselves full length before its dancing heat; Max, tired by the day's exertion, always fell asleep first, often curled up between the two deer-hounds where he hugged one or other of their sides for the infant comfort of contact. As his slumber deepened and he started to dream so he would uncurl and relax, sometimes unconsciously pushing his paws into the other dogs' ears or eyes, and sometimes twitching with such gusto in the excitement of his dreams that his kicks and prods must have caused real discomfort. But the great shaggy hounds seldom stirred; they just looked on with their solemn, mournful gaze.

Usually Max followed me closely wherever I went on the island and only when I was busily occupied in one spot for long would he become bored and wander off to explore the hundred thousand delights the island held. I never worried about his absence because I was free from the constant threat to every mainland dog-owner of motor traffic. There was little on the island which could harm him and I was content that he should roam freely and broaden the horizon of his experience. Often I took great delight in watching from a distance his cautious approach to some new object, a white stone or a spade cast haphazardly down in the heather, a bumble bee or the shrunken carcass of a sea-bird on the beach. His progress on these occasions would be slow and purposeful; step by step through the woody heather stems, smelling out each new secret in turn; prying into every nook and cranny; sniffing inquisitively at every little insect which hurried away from his stealthy approach. Suddenly his attention would be caught by something bright, like a sun-bleached cuttle-fish bone white against the grass; or a fiddler crab which had been snatched by a gull from the weed-strewn edge of a retreating tide and dropped from a height to fracture the shell. The gulls did this with a wide variety of shell-fish and crabs, dropping them time and again on the rocks and as often on the grass or heather where they never cracked but were lost or eventually discarded in despair. Max would stiffen suddenly, his whole attention fixed upon the unoffending shell; his nose twitching nervously to catch and store away in his growing memory any scent, any delicate taint which might reveal an identity; his velvet ears forward to catch the faintest rustle of movement and the loose folds of his brow puckered in enquiry and suspicion. Then he would approach, carefully, cautiously, every muscle tensed for instant retreat; first from one side then from another until he was poised over the shell, legs braced, nose stretching out quivering with curiosity. Then came the final, ultimate test of courage – actual contact. Sometimes that first delicate touch would stir the object from its resting place, and Max, unable to comprehend that it was he who had caused it to move, would spring back in alarm and, at a safe distance, sit clumsily down to eye it, ears up, head cocked first to one side then the other until his fear gradually subsided and he could begin his cautious approach all over again. When, at last, he had completely conquered all fear of an object he would gingerly pick it up in his mouth and come trotting back to me to place it triumphantly at my feet.

Scent, I discovered, was an important factor in the assessment of the danger an unknown object might contain. Items like shells, polythene bags, corks, empty bottles and other comparatively scentless flotsam were approached and invariably conquered in the manner I have described; but other, more odorous delicacies, particularly decaying corpses, were treated with far greater respect. The natural turnover in life in and around the sea is colossal, and the beaches all round the island held long lines of offensive and fly-covered sea-weed in which were often concealed the nauseous decaying corpses of marine animals large and small, birds and fish, crustaceans and molluscs, echinoderms and mammals. After a short Hebridean storm the piles of old dry weed would be covered with fresh, slimy wrack and tangle; long leathery strands of olive-brown thong-weed and, wrenched from deeper water, the intricate lace-lattice fronds of the red weeds. Examining these fresh deposits we often found common starfish sprawled across the wreckage like broken Christmas tree decorations; or glassy-eyed sand-eels, their silver skin dull and wrinkled in death; and the little black guillemot or oystercatcher dishevelled and crumpled, bright orange bill and splendid black and white barred plumage strangely motionless while luckier survivors of the storm sprinted over the rocks shrilly piping to their lost fellow; and once we found, rocking helplessly at the water's edge, the flaccid cigar-shaped corpse of a common seal.

It is almost impossible for us to appreciate the full significance of scent to a dog whose senses are entirely dominated by his nose. Touch is of enormous importance to us and the final analysis of almost every inspection relies upon handling the object concerned. We are naturally attracted to things which feel pleasant, fur, soft materials and smooth surfaces, and are repulsed by those which feel nasty: slugs, soggy objects and things coarse to the touch. If a child is offered a steel ball-bearing or a coarse nugget of gold the ball-bearing will be chosen every time, touch being the deciding sense. So it is with scent to a dog. It is the smell of an object which tells a dog what touch tells us: whether a thing is pleasant or unpleasant, edible or inedible, acceptable or unacceptable. We give our dogs playthings which are attractive to us, balls, rattles or squeaky rubber animals, and they are partially acceptable to the dog because they move or make a sound; but the toys a dog chooses for himself are seldom in the same category; they are more likely to be old bones, the wing of a dead bird or a rabbit's foot; in short, anything which smells good regardless of shape, texture or appearance.

At this experimental stage Max's repertoire of immediately recognizable smells was very limited and every new smell had to be approached with extreme care. Dead birds on the beach were a regular source of curiosity and he would spend long hours picking his way through the tide-line debris sniffing out this and that. He seldom actually touched a corpse; that was unnecessary; the ripe smell told him it was a corpse; and if it was so freshly dead that it smelt alive, he would bark at it angrily in a vain attempt to stir it back to life. One day whilst walking over the barren, fenceless moorland at the foot of the towering Cuillen, Max suddenly froze in a text-book gun-dog 'set', forepaw raised, nose into the wind and tail straight and rigid, level with the line of his back. He was about twenty yards away to my right where he had been running parallel to a deep dyke cut in the peat. I imagined that there might be a small covey of grouse crouching in the heather beyond the dyke, and I urged Max on to flush them out. But he chose not to move and remained stiffly poised as if transfixed by some strange hypnotic power. I walked over to him continually urging him forward to flush the game. He remained still until I was right up to him; then he barked, sharply and loudly. I was intrigued to know what was the cause, so walked forward in the direction of his point. Only then did he move, apprehensively dogging my heels and peering cautiously round me. We approached the dyke and there grotesquely distorted by the throes of very recent death, lay an enormous Highland cow, its eyes rolled to the heavens and its tongue lolling hideously from the side of its mouth. The story of its fate was plainly written in the deep black ruts in the dyke wall where it had slipped, possibly while stretching down to drink or on the point of springing across. It had fallen heavily and clumsily, almost somersaulting to land half on its back, half on its side, with one fore-leg clearly broken and twisted beneath the great hulk of its body. And there it had struggled until death had overtaken it. The peat sides of the ditch were deeply scored by the thrashing of its savage four-foot spread of horns; and its golden, shaggy coat was stained with the dark stagnant ooze and spattered with saliva. But so recently had it died that Max would not accept its rigid pose. He barked at it angrily from my side as if by doing so he could make it heave and stagger out of the mud to snort and stamp and toss its mighty head at him as did the others on the moor.

There were times on the island when Max deserted me and ran off to seek amusement elsewhere. Usually he went first to find Hazel and Dirk and if the two old hounds were asleep in the sun he would wander off to find some more cooperative playmate. Often he would tire of amusing himself after only a short while and come bounding back to Taichat and burst in through the door, breathless and happy. Occasionally, however, he would exhaust himself in play on some distant headland and, like a child, curl up in the heather and fall into a deep infant sleep. Before long I would miss him and step outside to whistle, and seconds later I would see the heather waving wildly as he charged across the island and raced up to me with a greeting which only at least three months' absence would merit. Once, however, my repeated whistling failed to bring him to me and I began to worry. After an hour of whistling, calling and searching all round the island I was in the depths of despair. I felt sure that he must have slipped and fallen among the rocks somewhere and was lying injured or even dead in some dark tidal hollow where I would never find him; or that he had fallen into the water and been sucked out to sea by the seven-knot current which passed through the island straits.

There was a brisk wind that day and I recall being worried in case I should not hear his injured cries. I tried to remember where and when I had last seen him. We had taken the launch over to Kyle for diesel fuel and Max sat happily on the bows all the way there and back. When we arrived back at the jetty I remembered seeing him leap ashore and bound off to greet Hazel and Dirk while Donald and I unloaded the drums of fuel. Donald had then returned the launch to her mooring twenty-five yards off the front of the island, and I had gone on up to the house to write up the fuel log.

Three hours passed, still without trace or clue. Donald and Willie had joined in the search and we had combed the entire tidal zone all round the island. We decided to take the dinghy and the launch out and search the surrounding islands in case the current had swept him close enough to one of them to struggle ashore. We pushed off in the dinghy in solemn silence. It seemed a forlorn hope that I would ever see him again, and for the first time I began to realize how much he meant to me. The dinghy bored round the front of the island to where the *Amara* was moored. Then, as we approached the launch, a little white face appeared over the gunwale. I felt momentarily sick with relief and could find no words to applaud that moment. As we drew alongside, Max leapt down into the dinghy, wriggling, dancing, jumping and prancing about the boat in ecstasy at our reunion. He had re-boarded the *Amara* unseen when she stood at the jetty, and Donald had returned the boat to her mooring without realizing that Max was on board. He had been marooned there for over four hours and his piteous cries had been carried away from the island by the breeze.

SEVEN

The Journey Home

By the end of August I was pleased with the progress we were making on the island zoo. The weather had been kind and we had been able to work outside late into the evenings so that some days we had worked for fourteen hours without realizing it. The bird of prey aviaries we were building behind the house were almost complete and looked most impressive against the rock face they were ranged along. Gavin had hoped to build up a collection of hand-reared hawks and falcons, procured either from friends or imported. The birds could be flown from the fist, or displayed on blocks on days when the island was open to the public. The idea of a hawk or a falcon kept permanently in an aviary was repugnant to us both. Nevertheless, the aviaries we had built were the most suitable I have seen outside the Regent's Park Zoo. The rock face at the back provided shelter and many fissures and ledges to perch on; and the flight space, a 30 ft × 20 ft ground area by 14 ft high allowed room for movement and exercise.

Besides these we had netted in large areas of flat heather on the top of the island to enclose grouse and black-game. We had used a fine nylon netting which was almost invisible against the background of the sea so that from certain observation points visitors would be able to watch the birds in their natural surroundings without the 'zoo' experience of peering through wire-netting or bars. The project was taking shape before our eyes and as each enclosure was completed I felt more and more confident that as the animals began to arrive we would be able to house them adequately. Happily, the season for young animals which might be unwisely fostered upon us by well-wishers was nearly over, and the threat of the gift of a seal-pup or red and roe deer calves was now receding.

On 31 August we worked until dark and it was midnight before we had had supper and cleared away the dishes. Donald went off to bed and I worked in Taichat on the book for a further hour before turning off the generator and going to bed myself.

As I lay awake I turned over and over in my mind the problems I was encountering with the section of our book which dealt with Grey or Atlantic seals, and how to cope with the controversy over the official decision to limit their numbers in British waters by annual culling. At best it was a tricky subject and one obscured by the conflicting emotions of 'animal lovers' and those whose coastal fisheries were threatened by the damage inflicted to nets and fish populations by the seals.

In many ways I was out of my depth. My own experience of Grey Seals was limited and it was a section of the book on which I was utterly dependent upon Gavin for help. He had done much research into the problems of Grey Seal culling for his book *Seals of the World* which was published in the Constable World Wildlife Series in 1967. Without direct consultation with Gavin I could really proceed no further, and, since he was not likely to return to the island for another week, I decided that rather than hold the work up I would drive to Inverness in the morning and spend the day sorting it out with him in hospital.

The night was warm and still and I slept lightly, waking often and staring out into the dark. At last the velvet blue began to pale and, impatient for the day, I got up and hurriedly dressed by the light of a candle. As I lifted the latch and pulled back the door to let Max out, the dawn unfolded in a silent stream across the sea to the west of the island.

In mountainous scenery night can dissolve into full light very quickly. On a clear morning at Kyleakin the first hint of the dawn was a faint glimmer appearing behind the eastern peaks of Kintail and Shiel. For several minutes that glimmer would swell in intensity until the mountains were vividly silhouetted by the gathering light behind them, the land and the sea to the west of them still steeped in their shadow. When the morning finally spilt over the peaks it flooded down their rugged slopes like laval streams of quicksilver engulfing the whole scene and gliding across the surface of the loch with the ease and grace of a skater. In seconds the night was gone.

I worked quietly at my desk in Taichat until a more considerate hour and then, whistling to Max to follow, I walked down to the main house. The day was fresh, pure and pink-tinged by the sun; and while Donald dressed I made porridge and brewed pints of black aromatic coffee. That morning was, I think, the last time we were to sit outside, basking in the morning sun, happy with the present and careless of the future. At half-past nine Donald took me across to Kyle-akin in the dinghy and, collecting Burgess, my old car, I caught the Kyle of Lochalsh ferry and set off up the road to Inverness. I remember that with characteristic West High-land disregard for the calendar I had overlooked that it was an English public holiday and it was some time before I was able to explain the unusual density of traffic on the mainland.

As was commonly my habit on that journey I stopped in the sweeping trough of Glen Cluanie and searched the vast, desolate slopes for herds of deer. A bevy of Land Rovers parked on the moor some distance from the road suggested a stalking party and I scrutinized the hill with field-glasses until I found them; five creeping ants delicately picking their way across the gravel scree of a corrie, edging along an un-mapped contour of scent and wind towards some predatory vantage point beyond my view.

The air was thick and warm, stirred only by a gentle breeze which whispered in the heather stems around me and brushed my face. I was pleased not to be one of the stalking party, tweed-clad and sweating two thousand feet up on a hill; it was a day for watching, not participating. My attention must have been averted for some minutes after the stalkers disappeared from view because when the shot came it took me by surprise; a dull muted thud echoing from combe to combe, backwards and forwards across the glen. I rose slowly from the heather and dusted the husks of last year's blooms from my trousers. It was so warm and pleasant that I could have sat there all day, but, anxious to see Gavin I climbed back into the car and drove on up the road.

As I neared Inverness I turned off the road to visit Richard Frere. The drive swept steeply up to his house, a large white building on the hill overlooking Loch Ness. The front door was set in a small circular tower characteristic of baronial architecture, and as I pulled up on the gravel outside Richard came out to meet me. His face was unusually stern. He had news of an eventuality which, even long after its realization, I found difficult to accept. Gavin was suffering from an advanced condition of lung cancer and the expectation of his life lay within six months.

Over lunch Richard and I discussed the implications of this news, but inconclusively. The little world of Gavin Maxwell Enterprises had so absorbed us both, Richard for far longer than I, that it was impossible to imagine its existence without Gavin. We talked ourselves round and round in circles, each fresh circuit relying for impetus upon a foolish, groundless hope or the unlikely chance of a miracle. At length there was no more to be said, just as there was nothing more we could do, so we drove in to the hospital together.

However grave our mood when we entered Gavin's ward that afternoon, it was short lived. Gavin was fully aware of his condition and as far as I could tell had accepted it with a new and uncharacteristic fatalism. He showed no outward sign of distress. As before he was sitting up in bed wearing one of his polo-necked sweaters, again a bright red one. The inevitable cigarette smouldered in his left hand. 'Pour yourselves a drink,' he said cheerily as we greeted him and I busied myself in this task, leaving Richard to breach the moment of initial conversation. But there was no need for anxiety. Within minutes we were deep in discussion about his condition which he treated openly and analytically and with an almost embarrassing objectivity. He quickly revealed to us that far from succumbing to the situation he was busily making notes for a last book which was to be the autobiography of a man dying of lung cancer. The title, he had already decided, was to be *The Tunnel.*

To me, most surprising of all was Gavin's cool arrangement with Richard to write an epilogue to *The Tunnel* after his death. In effect, I suppose it was no more unusual than deciding on the inscription for one's own grave-stone; but to Richard and me, to whom as yet the whole situation was intolerable, and with Gavin sitting in front of us apparently as fit and agile as before this sickening news had arrived, it seemed an extraordinary request.

I have met few people in my life whose enthusiasm for living matched even one third of Gavin's. In him it knew no bounds. It was not, as with most people, a flame that occasionally flared up or that required a particular medium in which to flourish; it was perpetually burning. Furthermore, it was as infectious as it was buoyant. It may thus be more readily understood if I say that, after two hours of concentrated exposure to that flame, I left the hospital in high spirits.

We had discussed the zoo and the Grey Seal section of our book, and so vigorous had been his encouragement for both projects that for the second time I felt blindly confident of their achievement.

Nor had he been slow in making arrangements for the fullest occupation of his own limited time. He was to remain in hospital for a further week during which some new treatment was to be tried. It was clear that it would be unwise for him to return to the island, so he had accepted a generous invitation from his good friends and neighbours, the Mac-Kenzies, at Kyle House.

Kyle House is not actually visible from the lighthouse

island. It stands shrouded in a belt of pines which surmount Kyle Rock – the Skye headland due south of the island and separated from it by only four hundred yards of water. The house is of no great architectural merit, but it stands, like the rock it is built on, rigid and square and with the same air of primordial belonging. The gardens justify a far more elegant residence. It was here, in the shade of copper-beeches and among the colours and scent of numerous flowering shrubs that Gavin chose to spend his last days and to write his last book. It was an ideal arrangement : from Kyle House he would be able to supervise the zoo construction and I would be able to confer with him daily about the running of the island and the development of our book. At the same time he would be accessible for medical attention and secure in the skilled care of his friends.

That evening I returned with Richard to Drumbuie, his home. As we began slowly to realize the gravity of the situation, a feeling of utter helplessness crept over us. I felt sure that there must be something we could do – if only to assure ourselves that we had done everything possible. My limited knowledge of cancer told me that at some stage most cancers were operable, and so in desperation I telephoned Mr Stuart Lennox, the London chest surgeon who had successfully carried out a long and intricate heart operation on my mother a few months before. By a strange coincidence Mr Lennox was travelling north to Aberdeen on the following day and would be able to see Gavin on 4 September. Foolishly perhaps, we clung to this glimmer of hope. I returned to the island and broke the news to Donald.

The next two days passed interminably slowly. On the 4th I left the island at dawn, and at 8.30 AM I was breakfasting at Drumbuie with Richard and Eustace Maxwell, one of Gavin's two brothers. Eustace had travelled up from Edinburgh and was visiting Gavin in hospital that day.

At 11.30 AM Richard, Eustace and I set out to meet Mr Lennox from the train in Inverness. We all lunched together in the Station Hotel and at 2.30 PM went on to the hospital.

For an hour, while Mr Lennox was in consultation, we paced about the hospital grounds. At last we were summoned to see Mr Lennox and the resident physician. The same quiet, gentle voice which three months before had told me that my mother would live, now told us that Gavin's cancer was inoperable. Five secondary tumours dispersed about his body had developed and there was no question of his survival beyond six months. But it was not six months, nor even six weeks, but only two days he was to be allowed, and he never left his hospital bed. Gavin died at 4.30 AM, on Sunday 7 September 1969. I had seen him once more before the end and although he had become fatigued and subdued by the treatment to his lungs and by sedation, he remained mentally agile to the end.

On Saturday 6th I returned to the island, and when on the following morning I answered the telephone to Richard Frere I could find nothing to say. I remember only his opening words : 'The news from the hospital is the worst possible . . .' The rest of that conversation is lost among a hundred confused reactions which whirled around my brain. I do not even remember breaking the news to Donald, although I must have done so within minutes of replacing the receiver. My diary records nothing. We can have spoken little as there was nothing to say, and, for a few hours, the island was quiet except for the continuous rustling of the sea and the wind endlessly shifting around us.

The nightmare which followed was to rage for thirty-six continuous hours before the world's thirst for confirmation of the tragedy began to abate. By midday I had answered the phone to seven national daily newspapers, a BBC News Department, the local police who in turn had been receiving an incessant stream of inquiries, and many sympathetic friends in neighbouring towns and villages who had heard the first news reports. I sat at the telephone all afternoon without a break, and after the evening radio and television announcement the stream of telegrams began; messages of commiseration and sympathy, many from personal friends, many more from distant acquaintances whose names were unknown to me, and the vast majority from his reading public. Late into the night the phone still rang, and in the small hours of the morning as I lay on my bed snatching what little sleep I could, I reached out to answer crackling, trans-Atlantic calls from Americans, strained faltering voices, some scarcely audible or intelligible, who had felt impulsively moved to contact Gavin's home or his family.

The culmination of that nightmare came ten days later when a small party of family and friends gathered at Sandaig for the interment of his ashes. It had been his wish that they should be returned to Camusfeàrna, the bay of the alders, where he had passed his happiest days. The ruins of the house had, perhaps not ironically, been bulldozed flat on the eve of his death. Only a scar of bare earth marked the site and it was there, in the peaceful sound of the waterfall and the murmur of the sea, that he was finally laid to rest.

Before the short service at Sandaig we gathered for lunch at Eilanreach, the Highland home of Judith, Lady Dulverton, Gavin's neighbour and close friend. Some had travelled far and a pause for refreshment was welcome before the long walk down to Sandaig. It was a hot September day. As we climbed down the winding footpath which many of us had traversed before, and as the bay and the chain of islands came into view, a hundred memories of that walk on other occasions – in rain, hail, blinding snow, and in sunshine brighter than that day – must have stirred.

Of Gavin's immediate family, Eustace and his sister Christian were present; his elder brother, Sir Aymer Maxwell, was unable to come from his home in Greece. Jimmy Watt, the original otter keeper who had run the establishment at Sandaig for so many years, was there and so was Terry Nutkins. Robin McEwen of Marchmont, Gavin's close friend and the artist who had contributed so many drawings to *Ring of Bright Water* and later books; Dr Tony Dunlop, Gavin's doctor and friend from Glenelg; Bruce Watt, who had been skipper aboard Gavin's shark-fishing boat after the war, and had had many associations with him since; Kathleen Raine, the poet whose verse had adorned the pages of several of Gavin's books and whose poem *Year One* had provided the famous title 'Ring of Bright Water'; Richard and Joan Frere; Michael Cuddy, who had managed Gavin Maxwell Enterprises before Richard; Lady Dulverton; Mr and Mrs MacKenzie from Kyle House; Donald, Willie and myself from Kyleakin; and a few other friends gathered one by one around the bare patch of earth which had been Camusfeàrna.

The open air service was short and at its end a carpet of flowers, which Terry Nutkins had designed and which he had had made, was placed over the spot where Gavin's ashes were laid. It consisted of pinks with a single otter made of white carnations at its centre. The simple ceremony marked the tragic ending of a saga and the beginning of a legend.

EIGHT

'Or a Fox from His Lair'

Any attempt to analyse the period which followed would be as futile as it would be impossible. Outwardly nothing had changed. We had become accustomed to Gavin's absence during the weeks he had been in hospital and the only suggestion of alteration or redirection in the course of our lives came slowly; as slowly and at first as imperceptibly as the waning summer and the stealthily darkening evenings. It was as if we were becalmed, sails hanging uselessly from the mast; and, as the days slipped by without return of the wind which until so recently had bowled us briskly forward, we became gradually aware of a sense of abandonment and desolation which our own efforts to paddle blindly on did little to subdue.

It was clear that I could not continue to write the book on British mammals by myself. While the research I had done had in itself been rewarding and worthwhile, the text for the book which was to have been Gavin's part of the work, had not been started and it was a task I was totally unqualified to undertake. It was a disappointment I found hard to swallow and it was some weeks before I could bring myself to pack up the files I had so enthusiastically compiled and send them off to a friend who was working on a similar but less comprehensive project.

But the zoo remained, and there was still much to be done. It was this which helped us to keep going, and it was over the episode of the escaped foxes that we managed to recapture some of our former zest.

Until now I had dismissed their presence on the island from my mind. They had shown little interest in us and I was happy to allow them to control the numbers of wild rabbits. To vary their diet, Donald had adopted the habit of dumping unwanted dog meat and bones which they cleared away overnight. Often I found the gnawed remains of bones, bleached by the sun and abandoned on parts of the island the dogs never visited; the massive pelvis and thigh-bones of the ox; marrow gone and the splintered ends of bone bore witness to the power in the vulpine jaw. It was during the examination of these relics that I found the marks of a finer tool : the delicate incisor grooves of a small rodent, perhaps a short-tailed vole. I had never seen any signs of rodent life on the island although a kestrel often visited us, hovering, sometimes for hours on end, around the headlands and bays. I had watched it regularly through the telescope in the hope of seeing it stoop and plummet down to snatch a rodent from the heather, but its efforts, at least whenever I was looking, were notably unfruitful. I was anxious to discover exactly what rodent life was present on the island because, if there were rats and mice, I wanted to exterminate them before importing large supplies of animal food which they might invade and spoil. I knew there had been one rat on the island in the past because Richard Frere had told me the saga of 'Jubilee'.

Jubilee was, and I would like to think still is, a large brown rat. He, like the ram, was necessarily celibate and lived in a state of solitary monarchy, being at one time, apart from the sea-birds upon whose eggs and young he doubtless thrived, the only visible occupant of the island. It is probable that he arrived as a stowaway aboard a visiting vessel some time before Gavin bought the island houses from the Northern Lighthouse Board, for his presence was discovered by Richard when the conversion of the two lighthouse cottages was started in 1964. In October that year Richard moved into the premises and remained on the island throughout the whole operation. Jubilee was apparently unaffected by this invasion and continued about his own affairs until one day he discovered that his habitual entrance to the house, under the lobby door, had been barred. Perhaps a little put out, he set about making another hole.

Richard meanwhile, as the day drew to a close, sat eating in the kitchen which lies beyond the lobby. Unperturbed by the sound of gnawing he finished his meal and then opened the door into the lobby to discover the source of the sound. Under the outer door he saw a whiskered nose busily enlarging a small hole. 'Go away!' he shouted in anger. The gnawing stopped and the whiskered nose twitched irritably. Richard returned to the kitchen whereupon the gnawing was immediately resumed. Richard is the least violent of men, but on this occasion it was obvious that something must be done. Rats could hardly be encouraged in the house, so from the entrance to the lobby Richard called again. 'Rat, if you don't go away I'll hit you with a stick.' The gnawing continued. Richard slipped out of the house by the front entrance and crept down the side of the building to the outer lobby door. There, busily tunnelling, was the rat; a large brown rat with a long scaly tail. The rat stopped gnawing, withdrew its head and impaled Richard with a baleful glare. Almost in self-defence Richard raised the stout stick with which he had armed himself and delivered a crushing blow to the rat's head. Jubilee staggered, recovered himself, gave Richard another menacing glare and crept away into the long grass. That was assumed to be that. Years passed; until, towards the end of 1967, Richard returned to the island to make one or two final alterations to the house before Gavin moved in.

On his first day back, Richard laboriously knocked a new doorway through from the lobby into the back store-room. He fitted the posts and lintel, levelled the floor with concrete and hung the new door. The following morning he discovered to his annoyance that some nocturnal vandal had channelled a passage through the wet concrete under the door. He filled the channel with fresh concrete and gave it no further thought. The next morning, however, the fresh concrete had been neatly removed from the original channel. This, he decided, must stop and he journeyed to the mainland to borrow a wire cage-trap for rats.

That night he set the trap in the vicinity of the new doorway and the following morning rose early to inspect it. In disbelief he found himself staring into the baleful eyes of a very large and very obviously elderly brown rat from the side of whose head protruded an unsightly, hairless bump. The disposal of Jubilee now presented a problem. Richard had by now developed a sneaking regard for the beast and found the prospect of its dispatch unsavoury, a betrayal of his own natural instincts. He decided therefore that it must happen, as it were, by accident thus absolving his conscience of all guilt. Cautiously he removed the cage to the island jetty and placed it within easy reach of the rising tide. For an hour he busied himself about the house trying to pretend that the unfortunate Jubilee had been accidentally drowned. Finally, unable to deceive his conscience any longer, he ran to the jetty to see whether the deed was yet done. The tide had risen and covered the cage, but Jubilee showed no signs of discomfort in his new element and was energetically swimming about. But it was apparent that he would soon be running short of air and, unable to watch the animal drown, Richard pulled the cage out of the water. Again Jubilee fixed him with that malignant stare. Release alone now remained the only condition for complete absolution, so Richard rowed the bedraggled but still defiant rat over to Skye where apologetically he let him go.

I now knew the island to be free of rats, but I was not entirely displeased to find evidence of other small rodents. It was another link in the ecological chain and one which I hoped to be able to identify as the comparatively harmless short-tailed vole. They were also a further source of food for the foxes and I was not surprised to find that small tunnels in the peat had been excavated, and once I found what I took to be a nest scattered around the hole. Periodically I

shot marauding hoodies and gulls and left their carcasses on
the top of the island. Always they disappeared over-night
and a selection of broken and torn primary feathers and feet
gradually accumulated outside a gaping fissure in the rocky
edge which sloped away from the main island block behind
the lighthouse. This corner of the island comprised an acre
of massive boulders strewn like the ruins from some
mediaeval fortress sacked by giants. Out of the midst of this
rubble protruded a gigantic boss, a rock which I named
Mansion Rock after its dignified Georgian outline which
was often picturesquely silhouetted against a flaming sunset. But its solidity was deceptive; closer inspection revealed
deep cracks and fissures in its wind worn face, lines of age
dating from volcanic movements aeons past. Here were
strongholds for a hundred foxes and I had little doubt that
our three were already bastioned within its interior.

One morning one of the young herons accidentally
escaped. I say accidentally with certainty because before it
happened the bird showed no desire to be removed from the
company of its fellows and, on finding itself miraculously
outside the wire of its pen, displayed obvious frustration at
its inability to reverse the miracle. It happened as Donald
approached with the morning fish bucket. The herons began
to shuffle about, clacking their beaks in eager anticipation
and stretching their necks until they looked like umbrellas
with extravagant goosehead handles. One bird, perched on
the top of a large rock, decided at that moment to stretch
and exercise its wings. Unhappily, just as it raised both fully
extended wings for a final, powerful flap, there came a sudden gust of wind. Finding itself unexpectedly airborne the
heron squawked loudly in alarm, instinctively flapped again
and thus propelled itself over the wire-netting and on to
the path beyond where it landed with even less dignity than
when it had taken off.

While the herons had no fear of man, they had never
actually been handled and were quite unused to any attempt
to do so. The unhappy escapee stalked back and forth along

the wire stupidly eyeing the others, its head first on one side, then on the other. Many animals faced with unfamiliar and apparently insoluble situations behave with dignity or at least react in some way directly related to the circumstances. The heron reveals no such reasoning; in appearance it is a most stupid bird. Its behaviour, its imperial haughty eye and august composure, suggest an extreme right wing Conservatism, an absurd awareness of its own social superiority; yet, true to its human counterpart, the more it attempts to maintain its dignity in unfamiliar circumstances, the more ridiculous it looks. Whenever we approached the unfortunate bird it stalked off with its head in the air, disdainful of our vulgar offers of assistance, and as soon as we had gone from sight it hurried back to peer solemnly through the wire. In the evening we tried to coax it with fresh mackerel through the open entrance of its pen, but it would not deign to cross the threshold. As a last resort Donald and I joined in a combined effort to catch it, but its long legs propelled it down the path and out on to the rocks much faster than we could travel and we were forced to leave it standing among the pools below the lighthouse – ironically, in the bay which was eventually to be enclosed to contain the herons and waders.

At dusk it had returned to the wire and had settled itself to roost in the lee of the cliff face which formed the west wall of the enclosure. There I imagined it would be safe for the night and we left it and returned to the house. Two hours later, as I prepared to go to bed I heard the herons' penetrating cries of alarm. I ran out with a torch to find the four birds in the pen in a state of great distress staring into the darkness wide-eyed with fear. Of the escaped bird there was no trace. I searched all round the pen, down the path and along the shore but without a clue, and I guessed that the foxes had wasted no time in securing such easy prey.

Sadly I returned to bed and lay awake devising ingenious traps in which we might catch the foxes alive, enabling us to deport them. The temporary advantages their escape had provided had now turned sour on us and the problem had become one of immediate urgency. The flimsy wire netting of the herons' enclosure was intended to keep herons in, not foxes out, and I feared that now they had sampled the delicacy of plump young heron they might be tempted to add breaking and entering to the charges already on their heads.

In the morning Donald and I searched again for the missing bird – and we found it, or rather its remains. The broken slate-blue wings and delicate brown legs lay scattered over the sward among other relics outside a deep fissure in Mansion Rock. I put my head down to its entrance and smelt the musky pungence of fox.

Long years as a hill shepherd had instilled an active dislike for all foxes into Willie's usually accommodating heart, and when I described the circumstances of the heron's death to him he set to work on a trap with enthusiastic vigour. The result at the end of the day was an intricate and ingenious arrangement of strings and pulleys, sliding doors and trip wires, and the doubtful attraction of an old hen specially procured at the bargain price of two and sixpence, for bait. The cage comprised a large portion of the foxes' old pen and a wire netting extension tunnel through which the foxes must pass to reach the bait. So that hunger should not drive the foxes to the remaining herons we left out a selection of dog bones and meat which had been burnt by the deep freezes. That night we retired to bed eagerly in anticipation of the morrow; the result, however, might easily have been predicted. It now seems obvious to me that the foxes would never re-enter a cage which evoked only memories of captivity, no matter how tempting the bait; but the dog bones and the meat were gone while, mercifully, the herons remained intact.

Three times we modified our trap and three times we were unsuccessful. But on the fourth day the wave of destruction advanced a stage further. Walking through the heather on the top of the island I noticed Max's tail stiffen as he set into the wind, his body rigid with forepaw raised as he drank in the scent of game. I urged him on and followed him to a small clearing in the ling. Caught in the grass and heather stems were tufts of fur. The hairs were coarser and longer than rabbit fur and the characteristic graphite grey under-fur was noticeably absent. So the hare too had now suc-cumbed to the foxes' domination of our island. My patience with them was waning proportionately with their advancing criminal record. What little sympathy remained was only on account of their introduction by humans to the island. For this I felt partly guilty, nor could I blame them for behaving like foxes. But chance had brought events full circle and I saw no alternative but to ensure their humane dispatch by the most expedient means I could find.

I telephoned the local fox-trapper who was known throughout Skye as Foxy and who in the seven years he had been controlling pests had accounted for the remarkable total of 850 foxes to mention nothing of lesser vermin which also fell under his jurisdiction. Foxy explained that he had some traps on trial for the Ministry which would not harm the foxes but would hold them securely by a leg. I was interested to see these traps, and although I was suspicious of their suitability I agreed that Foxy should bring them over to the island the next day.

My views on traps are straightforward and are based on a country upbringing, a boyhood predilection for game-keepers and their odious duties and, in more recent years, an involvement with the natural history world and its peren-nial conflict between preservation and control. There are two types of trap which I find acceptable : the first includes any instrument of immediate and certain death, and the second is the familiar cage which holds the beast unharmed; but this can only be condoned when its use is combined with frequent visits either to kill or remove the captive.

Although there are those who would pursue it as such, trapping is not a sport in any but the most distorted sense of the word, and its ethics can therefore be much more rationally argued than those of hunting and shooting. Trapping is a necessity. The argument is thus refined to one of humaneness : whether pests and vermin should be permitted to die painful, lingering deaths or whether, as has for so long been the case, it just does not matter. Like politicians, pests seem to rely increasingly for popularity upon their public image. Deer, foxes and hares are current favourites, while rats (with the exception perhaps of Jubilee) sit firmly at the despicable base of the pole. Rabbits have risen dramatically in popularity since the myxomatosis epidemic brought its nauseating disfiguration to the public view.

I have long thought that the priorities of the anti-blood sport leagues are seriously misplaced. A fox dying relatively quickly and, in a sense, naturally by the jaws of a dozen or more hounds is, to my way of thinking, infinitely preferable to eight or more hours of extreme torture in the strangling noose of a snare; an incarceration which, at its horrible end, may mean a brutal, bloody death by ill-directed clubbing. Yet such savage brutality is deemed by the press unworthy of the space so readily awarded to hunting; and the patronage given to those organizations who would institute the abolition of cruel trapping and snaring is but a fraction of that devoted to the anti-hunting leagues. Legal protection for British wild animals is, as yet, slender, and what provision exists is virtually impossible to enforce. The savage gin-trap with its steel jaws is, at last, outlawed in England and Wales and soon will be in Scotland, but the law still permits the conditional use of gases and poisons which cause animals to die in searing pain and convulsions, to say nothing of the legitimate horrors of indiscriminate shootings. Snares, too, remain unrestricted except on deer and are openly recommended by some authorities. To those who have not actually seen a snare or a gin-trap in use, the words may connote some romantic myth of moonlight poaching and villagery. I have seen a golden eagle in a gin-trap, its magnificent wings battered and crumpled from continued thrashing attempts to free itself, its beak broken and bleeding and its leg raw to the bone where the bare steel had chafed away the flesh. It had been there many hours, nearly two days, and it lay exhausted among its scattered feathers, its spirit finally broken, ready to die. I have also seen foxes and badgers in snares and read the terror and anguish in their staring eyes. There are alternative methods of humane control available in almost every case, and if the humanitarians would draw attention to these instead of cavorting about the hunting field with banners and aniseed, our animal pests might one day be assured of a painless death.

The following morning Donald collected Foxy from the mainland at a pre-arranged hour and when they arrived I took him off to examine the foxes' lair. When he saw their stronghold with its many cracks and fissures he sagely shook his head and muttered something which I choose to believe was Gaelic. We returned to the house where he showed me his traps. They were a modification of the gin-trap, replacing the cruel jaws with a fine close-linked chain noose into which the fox put its foot, and the spring then pulled the chain noose tight enough to hold the fox but without damaging its foot. I agreed that we should try the traps provided they could be set within a few yards of Taichat door so that I would hear a struggling fox and be able to release it into a cage straight away. Foxy went to great trouble to set the traps; he scooped out hollows in the turf and laid them flush with the surface; the peg and chain were painstakingly concealed and the foot-plate finally disguised with blades of grass. The four traps were set in a circle round another two and sixpenny chicken. I agreed to telephone him in the morning with the results, and when the task was completed to his precise satisfaction Donald ferried him back to Kyleakin beach in the dinghy.

The first two nights were unsuccessful. Each night the chicken disappeared but the traps remained unsprung. It was clear that these foxes knew all about the Ministry's latest traps and seemingly they were not keen to cooperate with their trials. The third night, however, was more exciting. We caught the ram fairly and squarely by a leg fore and aft and he took off into the night in alarm, carrying away two of the traps complete with pegs and chains. The next day we spent on our hands and knees, incongruously stalking him through the heather in order to recover the government's property.

By now the foxes had gained some valuable experience in trap evasion but on our side the debit was steadily mounting. Plainly we could not continue to waste time and expense on their capture and so, unwillingly, I agreed to a more aggressive approach. Foxy returned to the island with his shotgun and a terrier, a knotty little dog whose temperament adequately matched his wiry coat. I joined him with a second gun and we climbed up over the island watershed to a rocky slope on the other side. The day was Mediterranean; the sea glass-calm and the horizon hidden by a heat haze which made the air thick and stifling. The midges danced around our ears in countless millions, and the rocks were warm to the touch and glared white and gold in the sun. The terrier made straight for the foxes' lair as we neared Mansion Rock, his stump tail wagging frantically. He dived into the gaping fissure and seconds later his excited yelps reached us from deep inside the rock. We hoped that the foxes would bolt from their stronghold and that they could be shot quickly and surely at close range as they appeared above ground.

We waited tensely, guns poised, while the midges feasted on our necks and ears. Still the barking continued, louder and fainter as the conflict raged up and down the granite corridors. An hour later the terrier re-emerged to find us reclining limply against the rocks, the sweat flowing in rivulets from our brows. Their stronghold was impregnable. For all his wiry temperament and dogged perseverance the terrier had failed to flush his quarry. He was defeated and he knew it. He sat himself down and no amount of en-

couragement would persuade him to take up the cause once
again.

Foxy had to leave Skye that evening to work on the island
of Scalpay for a week so I decided to defer any further
action against the foxes until he returned; at the same time
I undertook to put out food every night so that they would
have no cause to turn to the herons for sustenance. So
quickly did they learn where and when the food was put
out – always some distance from the house so that the dogs
would not find it – that on returning to the spot only half an
hour later it would be gone. This suggested the idea of
ambush to me, but it was a measure I did not pursue; like
Richard Frere with the indomitable Jubilee, I had some
regard for these foxes. Besides, only four years previously
I had reared a vixen cub of my own, an enchanting beast;
bright eyed, alert, inexhaustible and utterly captivating.
When she was full grown I took her to the Westbury-upon-
Trym Wildlife Park where she now lives in the company of
other foxes in natural surroundings. She taught me much
about her kind in the months that she was my charge, not
least her remarkable capacity for learning.

Only the fox has accumulated around itself such an extraordinary amount of folk lore and fable; no other animal
has so versatile a reputation. The stories range from the
outer borders of possibility to the fantastic and ridiculous.
The credits include supreme intelligence, resourcefulness
and cunning; the accusations, wanton killing and Machiavel-
lian villainy. Sadly, the true beast, the English country
Reynard, falls disappointingly short of his reputation. Recent
scientific study of foxes reveals a fair intelligence rating
slightly below that of an average dog, while such seemingly
artful tactics as climbing trees and taking to water to foil
scent when being chased I consider to be characteristic precautionary behaviour. The species has evolved a scent consciousness the full significance of which, we, being excluded
from the exciting and colourful world of scent dominance,
are not able to appreciate. To label such behaviour *pre-*

meditation seems to be vastly overestimating the fox's mental capacity. There is, on the other hand, no doubt that the fox has an extremely suspicious nature. Even at the slightest suggestion of danger a vixen will move her cubs to a safer lair; and if that danger persists she will move them again until she considers they are safe. In addition to a suspicious nature, foxes are masters of field craft : their ability to use cover, however scant, has often amazed me. When I lived in Wales I used to walk the hills at weekends and the sight of a fox basking outside its lair in the middle of the day was not unusual. In the long summer evenings I used to sit and watch the sunset from the isolation of some remote crag. There, in the safety of the mountain shoulder with the valley farms far below, the foxes moved boldly about their business long before darkness, the ally of every fox in less secluded country. On many occasions I met a fox, sometimes face to face as I mounted a rise or rounded a bluff, and I often marvelled at the way it would vanish into the rocky scenery, not to appear again sometimes for many yards. Then, perhaps, I might catch a fleeting glimpse of its flying tail as it broke across an open space.

A hunted fox rarely breaks into open country unless hard pressed by hounds. As a silent bystander, I have often seen a fox which has been stirred from its hideout by the sound of the hunt as yet at a distance, and watched it unhurriedly looking about it and testing the wind with twitching nostrils; it may then cross a ditch or hop over a wall and run quietly down its hidden side in order to reach other cover without breaking out into the open. These tactics may even involve taking it back in the direction of the hunt.

Accusations of villainy are, I think, more often justified than many of the delightful tales of resourcefulness and cunning. Foxes have certainly been known to kill every chicken in a hen-house and depart with only one, leaving behind a confusion of blood, feathers and headless corpses. Similarly, twin lambs have been killed and only one removed. It has been argued in defence of this that if time and safety had

allowed, the fox would have returned to collect the slaugh-
tered fowls one by one, but the case collapses under the
burden of evidence from farmers who have found lamb after
slain lamb, which have remained undisturbed for days.
Incidence of lamb-killing and poultry and game-bird theft
has become much more commonplace since the myxomatosis
epidemic so dramatically reduced the rabbits. Rabbits were
the foxes' main source of food, but now, like the stoat and
the buzzard, Reynard must search elsewhere for his dinner.

Perhaps one of the most delightful and certainly more
fanciful tales of the artful fox is that of a vixen who wished
to rid herself of fleas. Gathering a bundle of sheep's wool
from a barbed-wire fence she ran, clutching the wool in her
teeth, to a nearby pond where she waded gently backwards
into the water. To escape the rising water the fleas fled up
her body until the entire population was assembled on her
nose which, at that point, remained, with the bundle of wool,
the only part of her body above the surface of the water.
One by one the fleas sought sanctuary in the wool which the
vixen then dropped; she then emerged from the water leaving the fleas to drown. Alas, even the principle of this tale
is unfounded. My experiments with a freshly shot rabbit
plunged into the kitchen sink revealed a total indifference to
water on the part of the fleas. After an hour under water
they had migrated nowhere and appeared to be none the
worse for their experience.

Each passing day marked an advance in the boldness of the
island foxes. Several times I caught their burning eyes in my
torch beam as I walked up to turn off the generator last
thing at night, and one afternoon Max discovered one of
them lying up in a dense bramble thicket behind the garden
wall. He had never encountered a fox before though he must
by that time have been very familiar with their scent. At
seven months he was a strong, energetic puppy who imagined
that his only function in life was to chase rabbits. He chased
them all day, and, when the opportunity permitted, he

chased them by night. The bramble bushes behind the garden wall were a regular rabbit haunt, well marked with tunnels and paths. As we approached Max set off at speed, his tail flailing wildly with the excitement of the chase. The scent led him into the brambles and I watched his hindquarters disappear to the accompaniment of his thrashing tail. Suddenly the sound stopped; there was a brief silence and Max then reappeared, reversing out of the tunnel as fast as the brambles would allow. As he reached the entrance he turned and fled to my side. The fox, bent upon Max's immediate eviction, was right behind him and at the sight of me it leered, turned and vanished back into the thicket. I was surprised, not so much by its unexpected appearance and aggression, but by its size. It was an adult fox, rusty red with white facial markings clearly defined, quite unlike the sandy cubs which had escaped some six weeks before.

That glimpse made me realize that they were no longer cubs; there were three full-grown foxes running free on the island and if they survived the winter there could well be seven or eight in a year's time. I decided that I would not wait for Foxy's return from Scalpay but would take immediate action myself. That evening I shot two herring gulls and tied a long line to their corpses. I placed the dead birds strategically on the grass in front of Taichat and fed the line under the door. When I retired to bed I tied the free end of the string round my finger and placed a loaded shotgun by the open window. Perhaps my scent lingered on the gulls because the foxes did not come until two o'clock in the morning when I was deeply asleep. I had imagined that the gentle tugging of the gulls being eaten would awaken me, and in this I was entirely wrong. There was one almighty jerk which nearly wrenched my finger from its socket. I stumbled to the door tearing at the string on my finger as successive jerks painfully tightened the knot. Then the line broke.

As I write, nearly twelve months after the event, a coldly scientific reassessment of the whole sequence forces me to reject the conclusions I drew at the time; but they are, perhaps, worth recounting. As I knelt on the floor with the broken string trailing from my finger I experienced wild anger at my own humiliation; but deeper than that and more powerful, a sudden revelation which chilled the warm night air. That first jerk which had almost pulled me from my bed I saw not as the hungry snatch of one fox, or even two, but the timed, coordinated force of all three foxes – in retribution. When I had recovered I removed the broken string from my finger and crept back to bed. Then, filled with a creeping fear, I got up, hurriedly bolted the door and brought the loaded gun to my bedside. As dawn broke five hours later I finally slipped back to sleep. The intermediate hours I had passed tossing uncomfortably and churning over in my mind the uncanny sensation I had experienced, and the leering, mocking expression on the face of the fox I had seen earlier that afternoon. I vividly recalled being told of a pest officer who, inspecting a round of traps one day, had been attacked and horribly injured by a pack of stoats; a story which at the time I had scornfully rejected, but which now, and until the foxes were finally and unequivocally dead, nagged at my subconscious and made me stupidly jumpy. I disliked walking up to turn off the generator at night, and I started taking the dogs with me for the little reassurance they could provide.

Foxy returned from Scalpay at the end of a week and I summoned him to complete his fell undertaking with all possible haste. Two days later the foxes were dead.

NINE

Storms and Shells

It was now late September and the summer had begun to wane. The swifts, which had screamed and curved across the August skies, and the sand martins with their twittering song, had gone. But the swallows were still with us, rows of fidgeting head waiters, white chested, red-faced and immaculate in their sleek black tails, lined up along the telegraph wires and anxious to be off. On the island the shifting season had begun to alter the pattern of our ways. The prevailing wind had edged round to the south-east and the lighthouse bay, sheltered all summer, had suddenly become a cove of troubled, slate-grey water with angrily snapping waves which rattled the old iron rings in the jetty wall and slapped over the transom of any craft moored against its side. We were forced to move the dinghy round to the east bay below the house and haul her out each night, up the shingle in a series of two-man jerks, a yard at a time. All too often it was low tide when we wanted to turn in for the night, and we had to go down in boots and waders to slip and flounder through the weed-strewn shallows in order to drag the boat to the head of the beach where the night tide would lap ineffectively at her stern.

Neither Donald nor I had experienced Hebridean equinoctial gales, and we were caught rudely unawares when we retired to bed one night foolishly disregarding the uneasy swell and the thick motionless air. By midnight the wind had come in strength; the Taichat windows rattled until I thought they must break and the door heaved and shuddered against its bolt. I pulled the blankets closer about my ears and as I drifted off to sleep I remember hearing the first smack and splutter of fat raindrops against the roof and the glass. By five o'clock the steely glare of dawn found no lapse in the fury raging outside and, fearing for the safety of some of the animals, I dressed hurriedly in old sweaters and oil-skins and unbolted the door. The force which wrenched the latch from my hands and flung me back into the room was unequal to anything I had previously experienced. Little wonder that Max showed no desire to stir from his bed and I fought my way out into the wind alone. Somehow I closed the door behind me and with the rain beating horizontally into my face I half crawled, half stumbled down to the house. From the lee of the back porch I could see down to the east bay where we had moored the dinghy. To my hor-ror there was no sign of a boat. Huge waves pounded the strand where we had left her; there was nothing to be seen but seething spume and spray.

I need not have lost sleep over the animals. Wild creatures are adept at finding shelter and many seem enviably capable of shutting themselves away in a coma-like sleep when con-ditions are unfavourable. Owl was fast asleep in his barrel, a hunched and headless brown figure huddled at the end of his perch. The herons, too, had found shelter among the rocks of their enclosure and the gannet, also headless, his sabre bill tucked somewhere beneath one wing, sat happily breast-on in the teeth of the gale with the rain running in rivulets from his sleek and well oiled plumage. Crowlin croaked harshly at me from a dingy corner of his den, while Teko snored contentedly from deep within his centrally-heated boudoir. Of Ram and the goats there was no sign but I knew that they too would be snugly sheltered in some peat hag on the lee-side of the island.

From Teko's pen I struggled down the slippery path to the bay. The noise of the sea and the wind was overpowering. At times it was impossible to force one's way forward; the wind whipped the salt spray from each seething crest and lashed my face with a thousand stinging thongs so that I cowered within the hood of my oilskin. I could see nothing

of the dinghy. The orange nylon painter was still knotted to
the iron ring in the mooring block, but it seemed only to
lead down into the water where the boat should have been.
I thought it certain that the little craft had been dashed to
splinters and all her equipment, including the outboard
motor, lost. I turned and retreated up the path with the rain
thrashing about my ears and the wind forcing me up the
slope so that I was almost carried back to the house.

Inside, the air was strangely still and quiet. I ran through
to Donald's bedroom with water sloshing from my boots and
dripping from every part of my clothing. In minutes he was
dressed and pulling his yellow waterproofs over his sweater
and jeans. I unhooked a coil of rope from the store-room
wall and together we pushed our way out into the gale.
Donald was unprepared for the strength of the wind as we
left the shelter of the building. He walked into it squarely,
full-front. Like a charging bull, it picked him up and spun
him on to the grass where it rushed at him again, tearing
at his clothing so that he stumbled and fell several times
before finally regaining his feet.

Clutching each other for support we made our way down
to the bay. I wanted to find and recover the outboard motor
in the hope that it was not irreparably damaged; since the
water where the dinghy had been was of no great depth I
hoped we might be able to locate it and somehow drag it
ashore. To my surprise I found that the orange painter was
not trailing loose but was still firmly attached to the boat;
covered by the spume and the waves, I had been unable to
see it before. Now the tide had withdrawn a few feet and the
bows were just visible below the surface. I passed one end of
the rope to Donald and shouted to him to make it fast
around his waist. Thus lashed together we waded out into
the surging foam. Within seconds we were drenched. As each
great comber piled down upon us, we could only close our
eyes, grit our teeth and clutch desperately to the side of the
boat. A dozen times I was dashed from my feet. At one
moment the water was about our knees, at the next swelling

around our armpits as the suck and drag gave way to annihilating walls of surf. As I struggled to regain my feet, I could feel the whole shingle beach running beneath me like a giant escalator. Again I lost my footing and the next wave surged down on top of me smothering me in five or six feet of savagely swirling water.

The boat was in fact not seriously damaged. The storm had sprung up before the tide had reached her, the waves filling her with water, shingle and sand long before there was enough depth to float her. Thus, heavily weighted, she had remained on the bottom and the tide had risen around her, engulfing her but scarcely moving her from where we had left her the previous evening. It would not be possible to move her until the storm had passed, but it did now seem likely that the outboard was still clamped to her transom, so we continued to edge our way down the side of the boat until we located it. The waves had torn it loose from its clamps, but we discovered that it was still attached by a safety chain. Somehow Donald managed to unlink the shackle in the chain and, gasping and heaving, we dragged the motor ashore. Although we had only been in the water a few minutes we were both utterly exhausted. As soon as we were clear of the waves, we dropped the motor to the ground and flopped down beside it. Heedless of the wind and the rain we lay there for several minutes before we were able to face the slope and struggle up to the house with the engine slung between us. It was still only six o'clock.

It was to be three days and three nights before the storm finally blew itself out, and by the morning of the fourth day the dinghy was filled to the gunwales with shingle and sand, buried almost, on a beach which had a new shape and look. It took us all that day to free the little craft from her grave and make her sea-worthy again; to remake her battered duck-boards, retrieve her petrol-can from high above the tide line at the far end of the bay, and rig her out with new fenders and a new bailer.

We had been lucky. The damage resulting from our first

real storm amounted only to a few slates torn from the roof of the main house, a bent television aerial and an outside door wrenched from its hinges. We were both sound in mind, body and limb, and none of the animals had suffered. Equally important was that we had learnt a lesson by gentle initiation – gentle, that is, compared with what was to come. We were never again to be caught unguarded with a boat left in range of the grasp of a storm-whipped tide. But the incident had brought one uncomfortable aspect of our isolation rudely to my attention.

We were equipped with three boats. The eight-foot dinghy we used daily for conveyance back and forward to Skye and the mainland; a tiny two-man fibre-glass 'pram' which we kept for rowing around the islands in fine weather; and the *Amara*, the sturdy ex-RAF, twenty-foot launch with inboard diesel engine and fo'c'sle cabin; this, under Willie's masterful hand, I firmly believed to be capable of riding out even the foulest Hebridean gale. The two dinghies we kept permanently at the island, and the *Amara* was moored to a buoy in the sheltered curve of Kyleakin beach at a point approximately three quarters of a mile from the island. The folly of this arrangement was made abundantly clear to us when, during the three day storm, the incapacitation of the main dinghy meant that, had we urgently required to leave the island, the little fibre-glass pram would have been our only means of conveyance. This, as I later discovered, was as useless a vessel under those conditions as would have been a soup-plate. We were, of course, connected to the mainland by radio-telephone, and in the event of an emergency we could have appealed for evacuation by helicopter; but the telephone had an uncanny record of abrupt failure at moments of high drama, and it would have been courting disaster to have placed ourselves entirely on its dependence. Happily there had been no emergency as yet and the telephone had remained in flatulent but serviceable order. But I was not keen to put its reliability to the test, so I resolved that the *Amara* should be moved to a new mooring directly in front of the island where she would be more readily accessible in bad weather.

Within three days of the end of the storm Willie had fashioned an enormous mooring block which sat like a great concrete coffin across the stern of the *Amara*. As soon as it had set we had planned to move the launch to her new position and heave the block overboard with its chain attached. But on the morning fixed for the operation the wind blew up and we postponed it for a calmer day. It was a bad decision and one which nearly ended in dual disaster.

The wind was strong from the south-west and between flurries of heavy rain the day had for the most part been bright and fresh. Donald had crossed to Kyleakin beach to collect Willie in the morning, and although the crests of the waves running past the island had occasionally broken and both Donald and Willie had arrived wet from the spray, the crossing had been no more than mildly choppy. That afternoon I worked at Wordsworth's desk in the long-room, and the occasional bursts of sunlight which lit the grey waters in my view made me forgetful of the wind which by mid-afternoon was lashing down the Kyle at force five or six. At half-past three Donald came in to say that he was just off to Kyleakin to get his hair cut. I asked him to post some letters for me and, tucking them into his jerkin, he departed.

The route across to Kyleakin was clearly visible from the window and after about half an hour had elapsed I began to wonder why I had not yet seen Donald cross in front of the island. It was often difficult to start the outboard after a rain squall and I assumed that he had had to remove the sparking plug to dry it before the engine would start. Nevertheless, half an hour was a long time and I was on the point of going out to see if I could help when Willie came running in.

'Donald's away in the boat, sir!' he shouted, wildly pointing in the direction of Iceland.

'Where's he going?' I asked incredulously.

'He's away with the wind, sir,' came the urgent reply, his hand still waving vigorously.

I snatched up a pair of field glasses and together we ran out and up to the north headland. Again Willie pointed frantically but for a moment I could see nothing. Then I spotted the dinghy, a brown speck far out in the huge expanse of sea which lay behind the island, dipping and bobbing from view between mammoth waves of twelve to fifteen feet high. I focused the glasses and could see that Donald was rowing, not rowing in any particular direction, but rowing simply to keep his bows into the waves; indeed, if he had allowed himself to turn broadside to the wind, the first wave would have filled the dinghy like a tea-cup under a mountain waterfall. For the first time I realized how strong the wind was. It was impossible to hold the field glasses steady for the gusts buffeting my back and I had to shout at Willie to make myself heard.

Donald could not swim a stroke. If the boat capsized and he was thrown from it he would have little chance of struggling back to it in a sea like that. If he was wearing his life-jacket he might survive for some hours; without it he would drown in seconds. I estimated that he was about midway between the Crowlin Islands and ourselves. That meant he was already three miles out and in another half-hour he could be well into the Inner Sound of Raasay; in that corridor, six miles wide and eighteen miles long, which runs out into the treacherous waters of the North Minch, the seas would be fiercer still.

There is now no doubt in my mind that I should have phoned immediately for the Mallaig lifeboat. But through some inexplicable desire to shoulder my own responsibility I clung desperately and foolishly to the only alternative solution. If I could reach the *Amara*, still moored three-quarters of a mile away off Kyleakin beach, I knew that with the wind in our favour we could overhaul the drifting dinghy ourselves, probably in less time than it would take for the lifeboat to be launched. I ran down to the east bay. The fact that it was sheltered probably gave me a false impression of what the exposed water was like. At any rate, I shouted to Willie to stand by the telephone in case I ran into trouble, and I hurriedly launched the little fibre-glass pram. The tiny craft bounced and bobbed like a cork on the water but I clambered in and, pulling sharply on the oars, sculled out into the bay. A dinghy of any size and bulk sits in the water rather than on it and is consequently less vulnerable to the wind; but that boat, flat bottomed and virtually shapeless, was like a saucer. As I rounded the headland and met the full force of the wind, it spun like a top. I fought desperately to maintain control, and as I pulled into the wind with all my strength the waves slapped against the pram's nose and drenched me with spray. Somehow I managed to keep head on into the waves and foot by foot I edged out into the Kyle. Soon my arms and shoulders began to ache mercilessly; the bottom of the boat was already awash, each wave adding a pint or more to the water swirling about my ankles, but I was making definite progress and was determined to forge on.

Suddenly I felt horribly alone. The waves were colossal, great banks of savage green water which carried my little cockleshell high into the air and left my oars flailing at nothing as they surged past. Sometimes I could see the island behind me and the mainland away to my right; the next moment I was lost in a deep swirling trough and for all I could see I might have been in mid-Atlantic. I have no idea how long it took me to reach the half-way point, perhaps twenty minutes, maybe much longer, but I knew that it was half-way by the size of the island behind me. I knew, too, that as I neared Kyleakin beach I would move into the shelter of the Skye hills and the going would become increasingly smoother. Reassured, I pulled even more fiercely at the oars with a vigour which came not from my arms which were like lead, nor from my shoulders and back which felt in the grip of some mediaeval iron yoke, but from somewhere within.

How I would like to be able to write that my perseverance triumphed; that I rowed that little boat across nearly a mile of tempestuous sea; that it was my own fortitude which carried me safely to the *Amara* – but that was not what happened. Indeed, it was my renewed vigour which nearly gave me occasion to swim for my life; as I threw my weight against the oars for what must have been almost the thousandth time, I felt the blade in my right hand give way with a sickening crack. The oar snapped cleanly in half at the rowlock and I landed sprawling on my back in six inches of water.

It is to Willie that Donald owes his rescue which by this time had been delayed by nearly three-quarters of an hour. While I was struggling across the seaway in the pram Willie was sitting at the long-room desk with the telescope glued to his eye. He had seen the oar snap and had straightaway phoned the Kyleakin Ferry Office for a boat to pick me up. I, meanwhile, was doing my utmost to steer the dinghy back towards the island with the one remaining oar. In fact I was doing remarkably well and in a fraction of the time it had taken me to row that distance the wind had swept me back to within thirty yards of the island and would have blown me right past as it had done to Donald, had I not paddled frantically with my one oar and managed to drag myself into the shelter of one of the island headlands. Willie had rushed down to help me and as I neared the rocks he had thrown me a line and pulled me safely in.

A fishing boat from Kyleakin arrived just as Willie was securing the pram. In minutes we were delivered to the *Amara* and were forging down the seaway under our own steam with Willie at the wheel and the gale thrusting us forward from behind. It took us thirty-eight minutes to reach Donald who was still manfully holding the dinghy's nose into the wind. We threw him a line, pulled the dinghy into the stern of the launch and helped him aboard. Against the wind and with the dinghy in tow it took us an hour and twenty minutes to throb our way back to the island.

Donald's story was as simple as it was obvious. He had rowed out into the bay to get clear of the seaweed before lowering the outboard and attempting to start it. As I had guessed, it was damp and had failed to spark, and while he was unscrewing the sparking plug the dinghy had been caught by an eddying wind and drifted out of the shelter of the island. From then on he had had no chance to replace the plug and get the outboard going; he had grabbed the oars and tried to row back into the shelter of the bay, but with a heavy boat it was impossible to make headway against that wind. If Willie had not been cutting peat on the top of the island and had not spotted his plight, it might have been much longer before we missed him by which time he could have been out of sight. If he had failed to make a landfall on the Crowlin Islands, the wind could easily have whipped him up the Inner Sound of Raasay, past Raasay and Rona and into the North Minch, where his next chance of a landfall would have been the east coast of Lewis, across some fifty miles of sea – or perhaps the logical conclusion would have come long before that.

Soon after this incident, Jimmy Watt arrived on the island. Jimmy had been the original Camusfeàrna otter-keeper and in Gavin's frequent absence he had managed that remote establishment throughout a span of monastic isolation which had extended over eight years. After leaving Camusfeàrna he had remained in close association with Gavin and now, in face of a new and unfamiliar situation, he had returned to undertake chairmanship of the company and begin the sad duty of sorting out Gavin's personal effects. And with Jimmy came his dog, Peugeot.

With the arrival of this newcomer Max's affections changed abruptly. Peugeot was a Dalbrador – or is it a Labradation? – a Dalmatian-Labrador first cross, and a hound of considerable character. He was a big, powerful dog with a broad Dalmatian head and bold pie-bald markings, and within hours of their acquaintance Max had be-

come so enraptured by his new companion, who not only
played with him but led him off round the island on rab-
biting excursions, that his affection reached a height resembling adolescent infatuation. They spent every hour of the
day together, rolling, playing, chasing each other in and
out of the bracken until they flopped down on the grass in
panting, tongue-lolling and exhausted bliss. In the evenings when we gathered round the fire in the long-room, the
dogs stretched themselves before it in a tangle of legs and
tails, smooth-haired and wire-haired, black and white and
shaggy deer-hound grey. I have never known a dog so im-
pervious to heat as Peugeot. He was always in the front,
sometimes actually in the grate and often so close to the fire
that sparks landed on his white and ebony coat and the dis-
tinctive pungence of burning hair made us raise our heads
in anxiety. It was comic to watch Max, who disliked such
intense heat, torn between a desire of maintaining contact
with his friend and the physical discomfort such loyalty
involved. His expression would change to one of obvious
delight when Peugeot, thoroughly baked, decided to cool
off at the other end of the room, where Max would curl up
beside him with the contentment of a child.

At night Max slept in Taichat with me and Peugeot remained in the main house with Jimmy. In the early mornings I cursed Peugeot's very existence. Max would wake
with the light and thrust a wet nose into my face in a plea to
be let out. Often I rebuked him sternly, sending him to lie
down until a more reasonable hour, but as soon as I was
asleep again the cold nose was back in my face and after the
second or third awakening I usually staggered to the door
to release him. Then it was Jimmy's turn to curse Max as he
sat howling outside the front door of the main house until
Peugeot, roused by his plaintive cries, dragged Jimmy from
his bed to complete the reunion.

Occasionally I had to leave the island to attend to business
on Skye or the mainland and I would whistle to Max to
accompany me. He would trot obediently behind me as far

as the jetty, but when I came to encourage him into the boat his divided loyalties became painfully clear – an expression which degenerated into one of despair as we pulled away from the island leaving Peugeot at the water's edge; but which soared to fresh heights of rapture as we returned. Long before we were even half way to the island Max would position himself in the bows with his fore-paws up on the bulwarks like Dr Doolittle's setter, searching and sifting the wind for scent of his comrade. Even now as I write, twelve months later and six hundred miles apart, Max's ears perk up and his tail wags wildly in anticipation at the sound of Peugeot's name.

By the time Jimmy arrived the *Amara* had been secured to her new mooring block which had been dropped full fathom five to the rocky bottom some twenty yards out from the southern shore of the island. A bright orange buoy marked the position of the mooring chain to which we belayed her bows, and a stern line ran to a bollard on the shore to prevent her from pivoting in the wind. The stern line, in fact, served a dual purpose, enabling us to haul ourselves out to the launch in really foul weather when it was impossible to launch a dinghy in the usual way. The idea in theory was sound, but in practice it proved a rather more hazardous exercise than we had anticipated.

I had collected Jimmy from Kyle of Lochalsh during a lull between gales and after unloading his luggage from the *Amara* we took advantage of the calm and pumped out the launch. It was well that we did so because that evening a strong wind gathered from the south-west and the shipping forecast warned of impending gales over the Irish Sea affecting the Hebrides before dawn. I had learned to pay strict attention to these prosaic forecasts which for so many years I had dismissed as belonging to some other world. Now I crouched attentively over the radio as those familiar names like Dogger, Viking, Fair Isle, Faroes, Bailey, Malin, Rockall, Fastnet, Sole, Shannon and Finisterre, names which so few of us can place on the map, took on a new and urgent sig-

nificance. Gale force eight, the man had said, and gale force
eight it was to be; yet the beauty of that evening held little
indication of the horrors of the morning to follow. After
dinner Jimmy and I walked the dogs up to the top of the
island just as the sun was sinking behind the black hulk of
Raasay. The sky was alight with a wild, electric glory. It was
an orgy of exotic colour; the splendid finale of some magical
Eastern pageant, now gently, almost imperceptibly fading
towards the last curtain. We watched it to the very end,
the footlights dying to a deep wine red, until the black of
the night crept in from the sea. A bitter wind sprang up and
whipped round our legs as we turned back to the house.

The long summer evenings had been a delight and Donald
and I had often sat outside reading or had walked the island
in the kind evening light which had seemed stubbornly unwilling to fade. Indeed, when I had first arrived on the island
I had been amazed by the difference in time of nightfall between the Highlands and the South of England. In mid-
summer it was easily possible to read a newspaper outside at
midnight and on such evenings we lost all sense of time; on
many occasions we remarked that at midnight it was too late
to go to bed since dawn was only an hour away. Yet despite
the novelty of those evenings and the calm of the sea when
it was possible to overhear a conversation on Kyleakin pier a
mile away, the dark autumn evenings also held special
pleasures of their own: a roaring fire and the scent of sap
sizzling from the ends of pine-logs; the wind moaning round
the buildings; the warmth and sense of security.

That evening had been just such an occasion. We had sat
around the long-room fire recollecting former days. The
wind howled outside and the shutters rattled menacingly.
We had listened to a gale warning for fishermen in Scottish
waters before turning in, and, as I struggled through the
incipient storm to switch off the generator, it was clear that
this was to be no petulant squall. Taichat that night seemed
to be in the very eye of the gale. The walls shuddered, the
fireplace covers heaved with the pressure of air in the chim-

neys behind them, and the ghostly blue light from the paraffin-heater threw weird, dancing patterns on the ceiling as the flame flickered in the draught. Half-way through the night I was awakened by a violent crash which I suspected to be the scaffolding collapsing from around the bird of prey aviaries. But there was clearly nothing I could do so I ducked under the bedclothes and went back to sleep.

The morning brought no change. Donald was up first and optimistically set out to bring me a cup of tea, but within three yards of the back door the cup was snatched from the saucer and hurled away on the wind. When I finally summoned up enough courage to beard the gale I went first to examine the aviaries which I expected to find in ruin, but they appeared to have withstood the winds well. I turned in search of some other explanation for the crash I had heard in the night, and was not long in finding it. Behind Taichat, lying in the heather, was a two-hundred gallon galvanized fuel tank which, nearly empty of oil, had been picked off its concrete pedestal and hurled sixty yards down a slope, its inlet and outlet connexions being torn away in the process.

Two days later the gale was still raging, the wind at times had reached speeds in excess of a hundred miles an hour. We had made our way down to the lighthouse bay, clinging to the rail which had been provided for the light-keepers in days when the flame had to be tended by hand, and we had stood gripped in awe of the mighty thundering ocean. The waves running past the island between the lighthouse and Kyle Rock surged down the seaway like great green, white-lipped monsters; rank upon rank they passed in a display of massive, incalculable force; Poseidon's militia in the execution of some dreadful duty.

The *Amara's* new mooring was being fiercely tested. We watched the launch anxiously as she pitched and rolled, her bows heaving at the mooring chain and the stern line flexing and straining like the halter on a plunging stallion. But with the experience of sixty years in the Hebrides behind him Willie had not underestimated the weight of the block and the angry waves snapped at the launch in vain. By the end of the third day of storm we were sure that the mooring block would never drag, but we were alarmed by the launch's position. She had obviously shipped a great deal of spray and rain and she lay heavily in the sea with a pronounced roll as the water in her bilges sloshed from side to side. It was clear that if we allowed her to take in much more the engine would soon be awash, so we reluctantly agreed to brave the gale and pump her out again. Jimmy and I dressed in oil-skins, but only as a gesture; no clothing could provide protection from the wall of rain and spray we had to face. We carried the little fibre-glass dinghy to the rocks where the stern line from the *Amara* was fastened and, clutching the cable for support I waded out into the angry water to hold the dinghy away from the rocks while Jimmy clambered in. He then clung on to the cable as I hauled myself over the stern. It took twenty minutes to pull ourselves out along the seventy feet of cable to the *Amara*. Sometimes the wind was so strong that all we could do was duck our heads and hang desperately on until it slackened and we could inch forward again. Often I had to release my hold on the cable to bail frantically as the level of water in the boat rose dangerously high.

Suddenly, in a moment of peak drama when we were both clinging to the cable with all our strength, I caught Jimmy's eye. It was impossible to speak and we had not attempted to do so since we first set out, but now that we saw for the first time our bedraggled state and the pained expression on our faces, we started to laugh. The sight of each other crouching in that tiny boat, desperately clinging to the cable half way between the island and the launch in the teeth of a force eight gale, was terribly funny; and once we had started to laugh we couldn't stop. We laughed until our diaphragms ached like our arms, until we were almost hysterical.

With biblical precision, the storm abated on the seventh day which dawned bright and clear. By eight o'clock we were busy. The jetty and the east bay were heavily clogged with weed and we shifted many barrow loads often stopping to examine or recover trophies; pink and purple sea-urchins thrown up by the waves, their delicate wine-red spines protruding like pins from a pin cushion; star-fish lying like cactus blooms among the wrack and tangle; and gaudy, atrocious sunstars, fiery red and flamboyant like cheap rosettes.

There were crabs, too, little green fiddler crabs with stalk-eyes and legs flattened for swimming; spider crabs, spiny-shelled with pepper-red pincers and fiercely protruding eyes; and hermit crabs, degenerates of the sea-bed, squatters residing in the coil of the evicted whelk, or skulking in portable shells with one huge and asymmetrical claw jammed across the entrance in defiance.

But it was the shells which were the greatest attraction of all, brilliantly shaped and richly decorated, and with names as lovely as their design. Needle shells, Wendletraps and Tower-shells with perfectly spun spirals and points as fine and sharp as a marline-spike; cowries with a glaze on them like Chelsea china, and Venus and Artemis shells. And every now and again we would find large, flat scallops, crusted with tiny barnacles on the outside and smooth and shiny inside with mother of pearl. It was impossible to resist the beauty of these wonders and we collected them zealously until every ledge, mantel and sill throughout the house was cluttered with them. Even now I still find them, in pockets of old coats and trousers, in jam-jars and match-boxes; and in the glove pocket of my car I recently found a cowrie.

The days immediately following the storm were crisp and beautiful. The island was refreshed and the sun shone down on the white-crested water with a fierce new brilliance. It was a morning such as this when Jimmy left us to travel south to London for a company meeting. I ferried him to Kyle of Lochalsh in the *Amara*, chopping and plunging through the waves with a salt breeze that made the flesh tingle and sent the blood coursing through one's veins. Max and Peugeot, inseparable now as Laurel and Hardy, stood side by side in the stern-well with their forefeet up on the seating, ears flapping and wet noses thrust into the slipstream in quest of sport or adventure. Jimmy was returning in little more than a week and had decided to leave Peugeot in our care; but it was an anxious moment for Max when Peugeot leapt ashore at his master's heels. Having been called back into the boat he returned obediently and stood, momentarily forlorn, as we backed away from the jetty and, with the wind behind us, churned our way back to the island.

TEN

Gulls and Gliders

Jimmy's return to the island was darkened by the news he brought. Gavin's sudden death had placed a crippling financial burden on the company and the income imperative to the zoo's continuation had been indefinitely frozen. Even at this early stage our costs were staggeringly high. We were geographically inaccessible for the delivery of raw materials and carriage costs represented an alarming proportion of the expenses we were daily incurring. On top of this our requirements were extraordinary in many other ways; any wire mesh or netting we bought had to be of a gauge and durability suited not only to the animal it must contain, but to withstand savage wind and heavy salt-atmosphere which often necessitated special galvanizing. Our labour costs were disproportionately high too. Every staple and nail had to be fetched by boat from Skye or the mainland, and the nature of the island terrain, volcanic rock topped by peat beds of inconsistent depth, meant that every fence post had to be skilfully erected often requiring concrete setting. We could scarcely move without incurring heavy expense and it was now clear that with our budget slashed to a subsistence minimum, moving was out of the question.

With the suspension of the zoo the hours fell heavily on our hands. We missed the challenge of our work; and with the realization that this situation could drag on for months, I turned my attention to a closer inspection of our surroundings.

It was not accidentally that I chose the herring gulls which, apart from the resident eiders, were the birds most commonly seen around the island, for study.

As I have said, Donald was an experimental ornithologist and his methods of identification and description were quixotic; but he also possessed an enviable approach to the subject which would have done credit to many more accomplished students of bird behaviour. Sometimes his observations were fresh and valid and often strikingly accurate. One day after he had been watching a heron fishing among the rock pools below the house he turned to me with a sudden and characteristic remark.

'A heron's neck is really a spring, isn't it?'

'How do you mean?' I asked, uncertain of his line of thought.

'Well,' he explained, 'if herons had short stubby necks they wouldn't be able to make such fierce jabs at the fish, would they?' He continued without waiting for my comment, 'The long sinewy neck is exactly the same as my arm when I throw a spear; so all a heron is, is a glorified fish spear with wings.'

I remember feeling quite envious of his vivid imagery. But on other occasions his questions were blunt and apparently without forethought.

'Why is a seagull white?' he asked one day. I was completely floored and forced to admit that while there undoubtedly must be a good reason I did not know what it was.

'You might as well ask why a raven is black,' I said indignantly.

'All right,' he retorted, 'Why is a raven black?'

I think I managed to wriggle out of it by changing the subject, but I was secretly intrigued by the seagull question and turned it over and over in my mind before actively searching for a solution.

The island gulls were always with us, their raucous cries as much a part of the atmosphere as the endless run of the sea. They squabbled over carrion on the beach heads; they rose and dipped in the wake of passing ring-netters; they hung on motionless wings in the eddying up-currents off the headlands; they sat in rows along the roof of the house and yakkered defiantly at our activities below. We loved them and we hated them; they stole the fish from Teko's pen and snatched the eider chicks from their nests; we awoke to the clamour of their strident voices and we went to bed with the sound of our gunshots at them ringing in our ears.

But we were strictly selective in our persecution. The gulls we dreaded most were the great, guttural black-backs, the vultures of the sea shore. They plundered the downy nests of the breeding ducks on the eider island, often rising with an unfledged chick in their bills and dropping it from twenty or thirty feet to be killed on the rocks below. I sought the destruction of these monsters by all the means in my power for they threatened the existence of every breeding bird about us.

In far greater numbers but thankfully less destructive were the ubiquitous herring gulls. It was their music with which the island rang and which held for me a special charm. My childhood in England had been occasionally punctuated by summer holidays in Devon and Cornwall and the herring gulls' voices were vividly evocative of a multitude of happy memories. Often I lay in bed in Taichat in the early mornings listening to their clamour as I had done years before in little fishing ports like Mevagissey and Padstow, and with the sound came flooding back the rank smell of bilge and rotting fish, and the hearty laughter of bronze-faced fishermen; disconnected trivia, too, so important in a child's life : a town crier and his bell; a rotting porpoise on a beach; a gigantic conger eel which twitched and writhed hours after its head had been cut off; an old lady delicately making lace with the infinite patience of great age, and, curiously, HMS *Vanguard*, long before she was scrapped and two of her portholes were bought and fitted into the solid walls of Camusfeàrna. The herring gulls were relentless scavengers and thieves but I had not the heart to shoot them. I used to fire my gun into the air to scare them from the island when Donald was about to put out fish for Teko and the herons, but within minutes they would come wheeling back to perch on the fence posts and bicker petulantly at their loss. Indeed, to have killed them or driven them permanently from the island would have been to inflict upon ourselves a strange emptiness, like a silent film without its piano accompaniment.

And there were other gulls whose presence we welcomed and whose graceful features and flight brought added pleasure to our days. The common gulls – absurdly misnamed since even where they are common they are vastly outnumbered by black-headed and herring gulls – and the kittiwakes. These were visitors only, spending far less time around the island and roosting and breeding on the uninhabited islands further out towards the Atlantic and the outer isles. The kittiwakes were particular friends and often hung around the boat in ones and twos when we were out in the sound of Raasay on mackerel fishing trips. They used to dip gracefully into the waves to scoop up the fish entrails we cast overboard for the special pleasure of watching them feed. One bird became very tame and sometimes drifted so close to us that we could have reached out and touched the ebony tips of its wings as it hung in the wind beside us.

That so much of all these gulls' plumage was white was a feature too consistent to be accidental and I was irritated that I could see no logical reason for it. In the evenings I spent long hours thumbing through bird books old and new in the hope of finding an explanation, but without success. Even Dr Tinbergen's superb monograph on the herring gull afforded no real clue and I was forced to conclude that either the solution was so obvious that nobody bothered to mention it or that there was no scientifically accepted explanation. Gulls have been wheeling around our endlessly changing shores for some sixty million years, fifty million years in fact before man emerged. Little wonder then that these seabirds should be so ideally adapted to their coastal environment.

In true scientific tradition I happened across the first glimmer of a clue entirely by accident. Mooring the *Amara* after a trip to Kyle of Lochalsh one day I fouled her screw with the stern painter which I had carelessly allowed to trail overboard. The September day was hot and the water was mirror calm so that when I peered over the stern to inspect the fouling I saw only my own face glaring up at me from the oily surface. I returned to the controls and cut the engine; then, as the launch swung gently round on her mooring, I stripped to the waist and slipped over the side. Despite the heat of the day the water was cold and I pulled myself quickly round to the stern where I paused for a moment holding on to the rudder; then I took a deep breath and ducked under. The brass propeller was jammed solid with the orange nylon rope wound tightly behind the boss. I groped in my pocket for a knife and, as I began to cut through the rope, I was conscious of shadows crossing the surface of the water above me. I realized that in my apparent absence gulls were gathering to raid a bucket of fish I had left on board. Suddenly the screw freed in my hands and I surfaced quickly, appearing, much to the consternation of the gulls, directly behind the launch. They were a small party of first and second year herring gulls still in the drab brown plumage which they gradually lose over their first three years.

It was only several days later that I realized the significance of what I had seen. At the time I was watching a party of gannets diving in front of the house. Gannet-watching had almost become a vice, and when they arrived to perform around the island we all stopped work to stare mesmerically at their display. Sometimes there would be twenty-five or thirty birds diving almost vertically from eighty or a hundred feet up. Round and round they would circle, their long powerful wings beating between graceful curving glides. Suddenly one bird would sight a shoal and its wings would fold for the dive. The others quickly following, sometimes all together, it was a breathtaking sight as thirty white missiles rocketed into the sea. A few seconds later, having swallowed the fish underwater, they would

bob to the surface and with slashing wings launch themselves into the air again, climb to the right altitude, point
their sabre bills and stoop once more to the waves.

We never tired of this thrilling display and sat like school-
boys timing the dives of our own favourite birds with poised
watches. We recorded one dive of sixteen seconds but the
average was between five and six. Often there were gulls
diving too, herring and common gulls, not in the spectacular manner of the gannets but gliding low and suddenly
tipping forwards to enter the water at an angle of about 45°.
Sometimes they immersed the head only and sometimes
dipped right under to appear again almost immediately with
the fish clasped in their bills. After a while the gannets moved
on down the Kyle and into Loch Alsh and I turned my
attention to the herring gulls which were still fishing within
convenient range of the telescope. They were a mixed party
of white adults and brown juveniles, and I watched them
closely for some minutes. I remembered the underwater view
I had had of young gulls in flight and a clue stemming
directly from that observation flashed into my mind. I
decided to experiment.

The girl who served me a few days later in the toy department of a large store in Inverness must have thought I was
some sort of crank. I had a firm mental picture of the kind
of rubber duck I wanted to buy; but, alas, the modern bath
toys were sadly different. I recalled an elegant, archetypal
species of rubber duck; swan-like, aesthetic even in its simplicity. But those, I was informed, had been herded into
extinction by competition from a variety of gaudy and, by
the look of them, carnivorous species belonging to the exotic
genus *Donald*. I was assured that no swan-like or even
remotely gull-like rubber or plastic duck existed in Inverness. I stood for a moment in thought.

'P'raps a gonk will do?' the girl asked impatiently. She
thrust a hideous penguin-footed, owl-eyed and eagle-beaked
monster towards me, its mop of orange nylon hair bristling
with static electricity. 'It's fully washable,' she added, smil-

ing, no doubt at the prospect of me struggling with this
hybrid water-demon in my bath. I snatched up a pair of
Donald Ducks for which I paid the exorbitant total of fifteen shillings and hurriedly left the department.

Near the street door I spied a section of the shop labelled
'Aeronautical Department'. An idea struck me and to my
delight I was able to make two far more satisfactory pur-
chases at this counter. These were two balsa wood gliders
with a thirty inch wing span and roughly bird shaped fuse-
lages. I hurried back to the island and set about converting
my gliders into herring gulls with the temporary resurgence
of a modelling obsession I once cherished. The first glider
I painted a smart adult white and grey, and the other a
mottled brown. I cut two fingers off an old pair of yellow
rubber gloves and pulled their open ends over the blunt
glider noses so that yellow beak-like protuberances stuck out
in front. I then painted in the relevant details : feet, black
wing-tips and orange bill-spot. When I had finished they
looked remarkably life-like and I turned my attention to
the two plastic ducks I had bought. These, owing to their
grotesque dissimilarity to any living bird were rather harder
to convert; but since I was only concerned with their appearance from under water it was enough to paint the flat
bottom of one white and the other brown.

The first positive animal reaction I received to my model
gulls was encouraging but had nothing to do with the experiment in hand. I had put both gliders outside in the sun to
dry, and a few minutes later I was drawn from inside the
house by frenzied barking. I rushed out to find Max, who
had previously been encouraged to chase gulls from the
island, in a state of near-hysteria because of the refusal of
these gulls to fly away. I tried to explain the situation to him
but his training allowed for neither exceptions nor explanations; he pranced wildly round and round the gliders
until suddenly he produced a superb, textbook displacement
reaction. Out of the corner of his eye he spotted the cork
float of a fishing net lying in the grass a few feet away. He

turned and pounced on it with venom. Placing it carefully at my feet he looked up as if to say, 'Even if I can't chase these gulls away, I can retrieve corks!' I led him inside the house pondering afresh the mysteries of animal behaviour.

That evening I prepared for my first experiment. I filled the bath to its limit and fastened a pair of underwater goggles over my eyes. I then submerged myself gently and lay on my back staring up at the steamy white ceiling through six inches of water. I then placed the first duck on the water directly above my face. It was the brown one and was predictably conspicuous. The white one, however, was not. Ideally, at that juncture I should have enlisted help to simulate the effect of a gull swooping and diving over my face. Lying on one's back in a bath full of water is hardly the best position from which to conduct such an experiment; nevertheless, I managed to do it myself, and with sufficient success to endorse the principle in my own mind. White plumage, it seemed, was a predatory advantage, the fish being far better able to see an approaching brown bird than a white one. I was pleased with the experiment thus far, but I had overlooked one important scientific principle – that of water displacement. When I got up I discovered to my horror that I had, in the course of my investigations, completely flooded the bathroom floor.

My theory so far fitted what casual observations I had been able to make. I knew that juvenile herring gulls did not accompany the adults to off-shore feeding grounds but remained to scavenge the intertidal zones and the numerous alternative sources of food which abound wherever there are houses – that could easily be substantiated by a trip to the local rubbish tip. I also knew from my own observations around the island that when the gannets and gulls were fishing the surface shoals of fry the young gulls sat around in squabbling huddles while the adult birds caught most of the fish. But my frolic in the bathroom had done little to prove that the young gulls were actually inefficient at catch-

ing fish, and it was clear that I needed more evidence. I
believed that my gliders might provide it.

On calm days the water in the lighthouse bay was as clear
as a mountain pool and I often sat quietly on the jetty watching the myriad activities of the sea bed : a world teeming
with life so rich in colour and variety, so incredibly intricate
in structure and design and yet so brutal in the eternal
competition for existence. I spent hours on bright summer
days watching the shoals of little silver fry – whose fry I was
never able to determine; they were far too alert to be caught
in any of the contrivances I devised; just small fry these,
friendly little fishes less than an inch long which swam in
constant, impeccably spaced three-dimensional formation,
every change in direction made simultaneously by every
fish in the shoal, until the plop from my carefully lobbed
pebble scattered them in all directions. Sometimes I threw
a mackerel head into the water and watched it sink glinting
in the sun as it twisted its way to the bottom. It never took
very long for the carrion smell to permeate through the
water. Usually within two or three minutes a common
blenny would pop out from under a rock and tug ferociously
at the head with all the might of its sinuous, olive green body.
Suddenly a fragment would break loose and the blenny
would be gone, back into the security of its cavern to devour
its prize in safety. And sometimes agile fiddler crabs came
scuttling along the bottom, half swimming, half crawling
in their eagerness to sample my offering. The head would
then be quickly torn apart and in minutes not a sign of
mackerel head or crab would remain in view. Occasionally,
a rare treat, a goldsinny wrasse would cruise into the cove;
a resplendent little fish about six inches long, armoured in
gilt and orange scales with an orange-pink dorsal mane
extending down two thirds of its back, a row of soft spines
intricately webbed by a delicate translucent membrane.
These fish swim with powerful thrusts of their pectoral fins,
forcing themselves forward with sharp jerks followed by a
glide until they are motionless again. Sometimes we caught

goldsinnies on the darrow whilst fishing for mackerel, but as neither the gannet nor the herons would eat them we used to throw them back again.

Towards the end of the summer another species of small fish visits the island waters. These, unlike the other shoals in the lighthouse bay were unmistakable in identity. Just as one can say 'starlings', when the sky is darkened by a huge cloud of birds as yet too far away for identification, so can one say with equal certainty, 'herring fry' when these little fish arrive, for they come not in shoals or in hordes, but in millions upon millions, in numbers comparable only with grains of sand on a beach or needles in a pine forest. Gavin had often spoken of the herring multitudes but I had never been able to visualize such vast numbers, so that when Donald and I first saw them for ourselves we could scarcely believe our eyes.

We were rowing in towards the jetty when the surface of the sea about us suddenly became alive with little silver fish; not just a shoal around the boat but a fairway of solid fish, fifty feet wide, stretching right past the island for hundreds of yards in either direction. We sat in the boat speechless with amazement as they teemed past us, the uppermost layer swimming so close beneath the surface that their dorsal fins caused continuous ripples; ripples which expressed an urgency immediately recognizable. These were migrating fish.

For ten whole days they streamed past the island and for ten long days the gulls wheeled and dived and the cormorants sat on the rocks like little fat clergymen in gorged repletion.

During this period I was able to observe the successes and failures of the diving herring gulls, and I was sure that while the young birds were clearly catching fish, indeed they could scarcely help it, the adults were enjoying a higher standard of success.

I had weighted my gliders so that when propelled gently from the prow of the dinghy they rose sharply to a peak and

then dived steeply into the water, finally entering at about
45°, landing only three or four feet in front of the boat at
which point the reactions of the fish passing just below the
surface could be clearly seen.

I experimented with my gliders until they were so water-
logged as to be useless. The results were rewarding : my
white glider had proved a definite advantage in that the
scattering reaction of the fish occurred only after the model
had hit the surface of the sea; whereas the brown glider
was seen by the fry some split-seconds before it struck the
water and the fishes' evasive action was quick enough to
have saved them had the model been a gull. The principle
seemed to be straightforward and logical, a simple extention
of predatory camouflage, white being the lightest colour and
therefore the best against a bright background, from the
fishes' viewpoint, the sky. This seemed to explain why it is
that the underparts of so many sea birds are white. Not only
gulls, but terns, puffins, guillemots, razorbills, gannets and
divers, and, to a lesser degree, the skuas and shearwaters,
petrels and albatrosses, although it is noticeable and perhaps
significant that those species which have successfully evolved
other methods of obtaining sea food tend not to be so
markedly white underneath. Perhaps, too, this principle
extends to some of the fish-catching diving ducks like goos-
anders, mergansers and smew. The shag alone would seem
to belie the rule, unless it is that since the shag is a deep
diver, its black and green plumage may be an advantage in
the dim light of deep water.

My experiment was over and I was pleased with the result.
In addition to this satisfaction I was able to regard the
young herring gulls with rather more toleration and I even
began to feel some sympathy for their cause. I gathered my
scattered notes together and compiled them in the form of
a letter to a friend eminent in the ornithological world in
the hope that he might be able to verify my conclusions. I
was sitting at the desk in the long-room quietly completing
this task one afternoon when Donald walked in carrying the

current issue of a scientific journal. He walked over to me and placed the open journal in front of me. 'Read that,' he said, jabbing a finger at an article illustrated by a large photograph of a herring gull. I read it slowly and carefully. It was a report on experiments being carried out by a continental scientist on the ability of fish to spot adult and juvenile herring gulls when flying over the water in search of prey. The results of his experiments with model gulls in adult and juvenile plumage on pelagic fish in aquaria had proved the advantage of white adult plumage. Perhaps, it went on to suggest, this explained why young gulls concerned themselves with alternative sources of food.

Confirmation had arrived sooner than I had expected but I was gratified to learn that at least I was not alone in support of this theory and I was happy to accept the conclusions of one better qualified than I in research of this sort. We opened a bottle of champagne in celebration.

ELEVEN

Islands Foul and Fair

Now that our days were free, Donald and I took the opportunity of exploring many of the other small islands around us which formed the familiar backcloth of our seascape. Six miles to the west of Kyleakin island lay a low dune-like isle which except on the clearest day was only visible as a dull green smudge against the black mass of Scalpay lying a further seven miles beyond. We knew little of Pabay except that it was famous for its snipe marshes, had once been farmed and was at the moment deserted except for an estimated population of seven thousand rabbits (which Gavin had gained permission for us to shoot) on some three hundred and fifty acres of ground.

The October day we chose was bright and fresh and with our lunch in a basket and Max sitting in the bows like a figurehead, we loosed the *Amara* from the jetty and churned out into the wind. There was no need to hurry; Pabay was little more than an hour away even with the wind against us, and, with the whole day before us, we decided to throw our darrows out behind the launch and fish the six miles of choppy sea ahead. The mackerel shoals were gone, like the swallows and the sand-martins, to winter in the security of vast numbers in the hundred-fathom Atlantic depths off the edge of the Continental Shelf in the shipping areas of Shannon, Fastnet and Sole. But there were coalfish, locally known as *saithe*, and *lythe* (which in southern waters are called pollack) as well as various species of cod which were likely to be attracted to our tackle.

We were no more than ten minutes out when Donald spotted the familiar black sail of a basking shark's dorsal fin cruising gently towards us. We quickly pulled in our fishing lines for fear that the shark's great hulk might sweep past tearing the tackle from our hands as the hooks dug ineffectively into its horny side. Seconds later the huge beast was beside us, the dark shape of its colossal body dimly visible beneath the surface. I decided that if we were to do any fishing at all that day I must make it clear to the shark that he was unwelcome; so, as he cruised beside us, twenty feet to starboard, I flung the wheel over and drove at its dorsal fin with the throttle open wide. There was a bump and a rasping sound and, as it dived, its massive flailing tail whipped round and struck the side of the launch below the gunwale. For a few moments it remained submerged and I swung on to course searching around for its next appearance. It rose directly ahead of us about twenty yards in front of the launch, lying across our path like the hull of a capsized vessel. I opened the throttle again and bore down upon it with all the force our old diesel engine could muster. Seconds before impact the shark dived, lashing the surface of the sea with its tail so that a column of spray rose thirty feet into the air.

When we had first sighted the great black triangle of its fin I had realized that this was no small shark. Often we had seen twenty-foot sharks around the island, but this, as it now rose to the surface alongside the boat, I realized was the biggest shark I had ever seen. The *Amara* was twenty feet long and with the dorsal fin amidships the huge beast's nose and tail appeared above the surface at the same chilling moment. I stared at Donald in disbelief. Its snout was fully ten feet ahead of the *Amara*'s bows and its tail a similar distance behind our stern. However haphazard the calculation that shark could not have been less than forty feet long and was probably more. 'As big as a London bus,' I had once heard Gavin say, but the significance of his imagery had not then sunk home. I began to doubt the wisdom of our hostility as I forced the throttle over to its maximum and swung the launch away.

But the shark had no intention of permitting our escape. We had started the game and it had firm ideas about who was to have the last word. For half an hour we tried frantic evasive action. I swung erratically to right and left, I spun the launch about as tightly as her rudder would allow, I forged ahead at full speed, I reversed at full speed, but the shark never budged from our side. The great brown hulk was sometimes so close that I could have jabbed it with an oar; sometimes only the tip of its dorsal fin cut a thin ripple through the water beside us. Nine hours later it was still with us, but much had happened in between.

We decided that since there was apparently nothing we could do to shake it off the best course of action was to ignore it. I reset the launch on a course, now considerably lengthened, for Pabay and we approached its willow-green shore at a steady six knots.

A hundred yards out from Pabay the shark dropped back from beside us and hove-to while we nosed into the shallows and made fast alongside the stone jetty, belaying our bow and stern lines to old iron rings, red with crumbling rust, set in the weed fringed masonry. From the very first moment we set foot on that island we did not like it.

It was impossible, at that stage, to say what was distasteful about the place. The beaches stretching away on either side of the jetty were like any other, shingle with sand rippled where the tide had left it; long lines of storm-wrack emitting the usual stench of rotting weed and clouds of tiny, angry flies. Above the beach ran a bank of turf and rabbit-cropped sward pitted with innumerable burrows. Beyond a perimeter of turf and outcrops of storm-worn rock the island rose to a low summit on the north side, the land dissected into fields by drainage dykes long filled with stagnant sludge and so thick with reeds and bulrushes as to give the effects of hedges. Between the dykes the ground, with the exception of a small rocky patch at the highest point where a handful of twisted and wind-shaped pines groped at the sky, was one large bog. In places the land looked like pasture, but on arrival the yellow grass turned out to be reeds and the surface was incapable of supporting even Max's weight for more than a moment. Like the land and the stinking ditches, the atmosphere was uncomfortably stagnant and putrescent.

On the south of the island a jumble of farm buildings lay clustered together like toys on a large green carpet. We wandered silently among them and were uneasy to find signs of recent habitation and, more alarming, of sudden and un-explained desertion. It was a ghost-farm, a Flannan Isle, a stage set with all the props for a thriller. Here a barn door swung on creaking hinges; there a pail of water discarded suddenly in the middle of the yard; an open window and a fluttering curtain; a table set for a meal for one, cup, plate and a tin of peaches roughly opened, the jagged lid torn back and the fruit untouched in its syrup. In another build-ing, door ajar, stood a potter's wheel, newly wet, a bucket of clay and the marks where five large fingers had gouged out a handful. But where was the potter and where was the pot he had made?

We stood in the yard looking about apprehensively.

'I don't like it,' whispered Donald.

'Why are you whispering?' I whispered back.

'I don't know, why are you?'

I didn't know either and after a pause I shouted, 'Hullo, is there anyone about?'

A jackdaw clattered noisily from a chimney behind us and winged away. We jumped and Donald cursed. My voice echoed back to us from the empty buildings.

'Let's get out of here,' I said and we walked briskly away from the farm nervously glancing back as if we expected to catch a glimpse of some frightened recluse, a Ben Gunn, bearded and clad in weeds, darting from shadow to shadow, still clutching the wet sod of clay in one calloused hand. But we saw nothing.

The whole island was chill and deserted like a graveyard, and it was a few minutes later that I realized why. I stopped to examine a decaying rabbit in our path. I turned it over gingerly with my foot.

'Myxi,' I said abruptly.

As we walked on we found carcass after carcass. The ground was littered with corpses, every yard, ahead and behind, to right and to left, mouldering bodies, grotesquely disfigured creatures of some hideous hell by Bosch. The whole island was a cemetery of unmarked graves. Seven thousand rabbits we had been told, and we saw not one live beast except the solitary jackdaw, an occasional hoodie or greater black-backed gull jealously guarding its carrion; feasting on the bulging cystic bodies which lay in thousands all over the island. Little wonder the stagnant atmosphere and putrescent air.

In the two brief hours it took us to explore Pabay the full horror of the epidemic was brought home to us. One could appreciate here the enormous impact such an epidemic must have upon the many predators for which the rabbit is staple diet. To take just three : the fox, the buzzard and the stoat. These three must now search for substitute prey. The fox turns more readily to young lambs, deer calves, carrion, poultry, game birds and a larger proportion of rats, voles, mice and beetles; the buzzard to leverets, and a wide variety of young birds including gulls, plovers, shore and game birds; and the stoat almost exclusively to small mammals, particularly voles. If one considers the increased predation from just these three species alone, the cumulative effect of the myxomatosis epidemic can hardly be imagined. How does nature balance out the sudden removal of so valuable a food species? How can the populations of foxes, buzzards and stoats, to say nothing of wild-cats, pine martens, eagles, polecats and others, possibly remain stable? How many voles and mice are worth one rabbit to the stoat – and why haven't the small mammal populations been accordingly reduced? It is the almost magical resilience of the natural world to meet such conditions that makes its study so engrossing and which, incidentally, makes man's management of his own affairs seem so pathetically inefficient by comparison.

We left Pabay in low spirits. It is difficult to view the vile disfiguration of any animal, however injurious it may be to agriculture, without emotion, particularly one so intrinsically attractive as the rabbit. It was, then, almost a relief to find our monster basking shark waiting exactly where we had left it. The great black fin emerged from the surface as we approached with what seemed a sinister leer. I throttled the *Amara*'s engine right down in the hope that we might be able to slip past the beast without it noticing. Some hope. The game had clearly reached no more than half-time, and with as little disturbance of the water as might be made by a goldfish the enormous shark resumed its former position, twenty feet to starboard of the launch.

Just what satisfaction the shark drew from this association (for our acquaintance had thankfully progressed to no more intimate terms) is hard to assess. From a behaviourist's angle the interest the animal was showing in us is probably analogous with that of a herd of cows to a stranger in their field : plain curiosity and with similar lack of courage to make the final analysis. Like the cow, the basking shark suffers no predation during adulthood (with the possible but unlikely expectation of the killer-whale which will attack virtually anything), but retains from its more vulnerable youth an instinctive fear of beings and objects unknown. A fear, however, not great enough to override another powerful instinct common in the animal world, that of inquisitiveness. It is possible, too, that the shark received some form of attractive stimulation from the regular emission of shock waves from our propeller.

As we cruised away from Pabay, the island once again adopting its lily-leaf appearance in the great blue pond around it, we unpacked our luncheon basket. We could no more have eaten in the proximity of Pabay than we could

have sat down to lunch in an abattoir. We were thankful
for the breeze which refreshed our nostrils with sharp salt
air and the antiseptic properties of the sea-water in which
we washed our hands with unnecessary thoroughness. Once
again the day became bright and invigorating and our spirits
rose with the prospect of our next adventure.

Some twelve miles to the north of Pabay lay the Crowlin
Isles, the islands which had given their name to our carrion
crow and which formed another more rugged landmark on
Kyleakin's western horizon. We knew much more about the
Crowlin Isles than Pabay because we had fished their sheltered waters throughout the mackerel season and we were
familiar with their friendly cliffs and the glossy bobbing
heads of the seals which frequented their shores. It was, in
fact, from the Crowlin Islands that the seals came when, in
the course of their daily rounds, they appeared around Kyleakin Island and its archipelago.

The Crowlin Isles are really one huge volcanic boss protruding more than a hundred feet from the surface of the
sea. They are named in plural because the action of the sea
over millions of years has split the boss into two clearly defined pieces by eroding a fault line running due north and
south across the western quarter of the boss. This rift has been
enlarged to form a chasm half a mile long right through the
block the walls of which rise steeply, in places vertically, on
either side. The effect is to produce a channel of smooth,
sheltered water fifty yards wide in which a host of marine
life finds shelter from the nagging winds and currents of the
surrounding sea. Entering the channel from the southern
end at low tide was like entering another world. Immediately
the water became as smooth and clear as glass and the
myriad wonders of the sea-bed were as open to view as fish
in a lighted aquarium. It was a fascinating place and the
more fascinating that day after the repugnance of Pabay.

As before, the shark was unable to follow us into shallow
water and we left him, not without a touch of regret; any

fear of hostility had now completely subsided and we had
begun to regard him almost with affection. As we nosed into
the channel, I silenced the throbbing engine. The quiet was
strangely awesome and we stared over the bows enraptured
by the beauty of the waving weed and the shimmering gold
of the shoals of small darting fish like those in the Kyleakin
jetty bay; weeds from each of the red, green and brown
zones, and crabs of all shapes and sizes. All around us rose
the friendly dog-like heads of little brown seals bobbing in
an inquisitive circle like shiny glass floats. They seemed
almost human, with big round eyes and deep despairing
sighs full of the pathos of centuries-long persecution for
hide and oil. Few sights are more delightful than that of a
seal swimming in clear water. These soft, cigar-shaped
creatures, so ungainly on land, move through the water with
the ease and grace of the gulls in the air above. In awe and
envy we watched them twisting and turning, nosing here
and there among the weed and the rocks, skimming under
the boat and popping up again to explore us from another
side. Their movement was so smooth and seemingly effortless that the water appeared to part before them, letting
them through without resistance.

Lying above the tide line, in passive segregation from the
common seals, were their senior cousins, the grey Atlantic
seals; great flabby bulls with arched Roman noses and a
dozen chins, the largest well over seven feet in length and
impossible to weigh without a crane. These grey seals, among
the world's rarer seal species, were in the past hunted to the
verge of extinction for their skin and blubber, but have since
been fortuitously reprieved by the appearance of paraffin.
The demand for seal oil is now non-existent, and seal skin is
only used in fashion and luxury goods. In this happier state
the grey seal populations have swelled dramatically and the
species is no longer in danger. But, as has not infrequently
been pointed out, there remains within their breeding cycle
one ill-concealed flaw : grey seals breed only in a very few
places, and these, where they assemble in great numbers, are

unhappily well known. Unlike the common seal, the grey seal hauls out to breed, sometimes as much as 250 yards inshore; and the young calves, conspicuous in their white fluffy coats, may remain ashore for as much as the first month of their lives. Throughout the breeding ritual the grey seals lay themselves open to mass exploitation by which means, if man so foolishly chose, the entire species could be exterminated with frightening ease. Such, then, is the responsibility placed in the hands of those who hold the power of legislation over grey seal control.

But the seals hauled out on the Crowlin Isles that day were leaving nothing to chance. As we approached, they shuffled cumbersomely towards the water and disappeared in a flurry of sand, a ripple of supple flesh curving away into the blue dim beneath us. We watched them depart, one after another until the rocks were bare. Meantime, our forward momentum had finally died and we were forced to re-start the engine. The noise was uncomfortably loud and, with the screaming of the gulls and kittiwakes disturbed from the towering cliffs, the magic of the islands quickly faded. The water about us now was ruffled by our bow wave and the crystal wonders below concealed from our view. We ploughed on up the channel and forged out into the open sea, grey and unwelcoming, on the north side of the islands. The transition was as abrupt as it had been upon our arrival at the southern end, and, finding little comfort in the chill wind and gathering skies, we turned for Kyleakin.

Six miles away to the south-east a thin white line betrayed surf on the rocks of home. The lighthouse, proud and erect like a toy soldier, awaited our return, its benign expression clearly discernible even at that distance.

TWELVE

The White Island

Slowly the boisterous, windy days of autumn slipped past and the dull wetness of winter drew in around us. The first winter migrants, the fieldfares and redwings, had come to the island in late September; they had filled the air with their hysterical fluting song, and had moved on south to their wintering grounds in England and the Continent. On Skye the birch and alder leaves had turned to yellow and gold with the first cold nights, and the Cuillin hills and the Five Sisters of Kintail were now capped with snow above two thousand feet.

But it was not these symptoms which brought the waning season to our notice; it was the steady beat of wings and the honking voices of the geese which warned us of the proximity of winter. First came the white-fronts, high in the sky in long, wide V-formation, twenty or thirty birds strong, each taking full advantage of the broken air stream from the bird directly ahead, the leader shifting and changing with those on either side to ease the strain of the front position. White-fronted geese first cross Kyleakin about mid-October, their voices filling the air long before the formation comes into view, wings in step, so to speak, dark silhouettes against a lead-grey sky. These are the vanguard, the front rank of thousands yet to come. Soon afterwards follow the greylags, less orderly, in long straggling skeins, their clamour wild and evocative at dawn and dusk as they forge south, invisible against the hills.

At first we rushed out at the sound, often leaving break-fast porridge or coffee to chill while we stared skywards enthralled by their music. But as the days slipped by, the sound came more and more frequently so that we no longer jumped up to watch them pass, but merely paused in what we were doing to listen for a moment as if in observance of some sacred rite.

And with the sound of the geese came other seasonal sounds, which, when the wind was still, echoed across from Skye. October had brought the red deer stags to their rutting stands, and the nights had been loud with their melancholy roaring. And from the corries high in the hills the mist and rain had gathered in the burn heads and filled the air with the sound of crashing water, million upon millions of gallons cascading down in great white spirals hurling before them boulder and branch. By November every burn and stream was in spate, a torrent of peat-brown water smashed into foam and spray. Every mountain slope was dissected by long white lines and the sound was incessant about our ears.

It was in early November when the only bird song around the island was that of the gulls and the passing geese, that I awoke one morning to hear a new and unfamiliar song, a soft trilling chatter like some rare cage-bird, but in force, so to speak, uttered by many birds together. I rose quickly, anxious to discover the source, and was delighted and surprised to find the rowan tree in Teko's garden alive with waxwings. There were about thirty birds, no doubt en route to a more suitable wintering ground. Indeed, to liken them to cage-birds was in a sense accurate for they outclassed in appearance all our resident song-birds. And they knew it too. They perched arrogantly in the uppermost branches, plain for the world to admire, vainly preening their red and yellow wing flashes and cocking their prominent nut-brown crests. By mid-day they were off, in long sweeping undulations, heading east for the mainland; thirty flashes of scarlet and gold as they disappeared into the brown of the landscape.

So the winter was on us. The eiders were rare visitors now, spending the days far out to sea safe from the seething rocks around the islands and appearing only on calm days when the wind dropped; but even then they were wild, restless like the sea, flying in low over the waves and pitching in twos and threes only to move off again minutes later, no longer interested in their breeding island. Everything that moved did so with an air of restless urgency as if some great calamity were at hand and there was no time to linger and idle as there had been a month before. Red-throated divers passed in high rapid flight uttering their persistent angry cry over and over again as if they were late for some pressing engagement; a school of bottle-nosed dolphins passed one day, sweeping along at colossal speed, breaking from the surface in shallow, curving arcs and sighing audibly as they went; a strange melancholy sound as if they had witnessed some awful tragedy and were hurrying away in alarm. The seals were shy, too, no longer bobbing about us as we ferried to and fro in the boats, but glancing momentarily from a distance and then diving busily to pursue their under-water lives unwatched.

The days were short and timid like the animals around us. At nine o'clock the light was still dim from the long night, and by five in the afternoon darkness was on us again. To pretend that there was any joy in these twilit days would be untrue. We left our beds unwillingly and returned happily to them soon after supper; and, at this time of greatest need, as if it too were loth to work, the island generator failed us.

Our every comfort depended on that diesel engine : our light, heating and hot water, without which our lives became misery. The trouble started when, after being stormbound for five successive days, we ran out of fuel. It was a further three days before we were able to cross to Kyle of Lochalsh to replenish our tanks. The trip was a nightmare. The launch jolted and shuddered against the pier at Kyle while the drums were being filled, and we were liberally splashed with oil. It was in our hair and on our boots and jerseys. On the return journey the waves broke over our bows making us wetter and colder with stinging salt spray. Landing the forty gallon drums at the jetty from the heaving launch was a feat of strength and determination by the end of which we were exhausted and drenched to our shivering skins. Then, to our dismay, the engine refused to fire. Water from the bottom of the tank had run down into the filters and the fresh fuel had forced it into the chambers.

In the dim light of torches I stripped the engine down and in doing so accidentally damaged a vital gasket. It was a week before the new gasket arrived. A week of purgatory. No hot water to bath in and wash the diesel slime from our hands and bodies. No light except that of rapidly expiring torches and tallow candles which dripped hot wax and blew out just when their feeble light was needed most. And no heating to keep the salt-impregnated walls of the house dry; only the spluttering warmth of the fires we desperately coaxed to life from sodden peat. Every day of that week it rained, and each day seemed wetter and colder than the one before. Every last ounce of romance was drained from the life of the island, wrung even, from us until at last, two tired, dirty and bedraggled figures pushed off in the dinghy and retired in desperation to the sanctuary of Kyle House. How welcome that bath, those warm dry sheets and the inevitable culinary delights of the MacKenzies' kitchen.

No one would suggest that life on a Hebridean island is all harmony and delight, an endless round of balmy days and spectacular sunsets couched in the deceptive tranquillity of a few high summer days. The truth is far removed. There are times when one is strangely at odds with one's environment, during which one begins to doubt the gilt of the first joy. To live on an island is to lay oneself open to all the horrors of the elements; it is to have to be self-sufficient in all those comforts we so often take for granted. And yet the magic of the first joy persists. The Hebrides are a drug to be shunned at all costs unless one is prepared for permanent addiction. The highlights remain long after the cold and the wet, the disappointments and disillusionments are all forgotten.

It is again December and the year has turned once, full circle, since Donald and I pushed off from the island bay, the dinghy overladen with our possessions, for the last time. That day was like today, cold and grey, the dinghy's ropes stiff with the cold and the air still with the silence of a winter morning. We were the last to leave, the animals having gone before, and the island had about it the unwelcoming chill of an empty house. The final decision had come suddenly. There were at that time crippling financial obligations which could be made soluble only by the sale of the island property.

The news had come as no surprise to us. The remaining strands of hope for the continuation of the zoo had been severed one by one, and by the time they finally snapped altogether we accepted it with little or no feeling. Then, while the property was on the market, began the wearisome task of dismantling the sections of the jig-saw we had so carefully pieced together. But there were joys even in that ostensibly depressing duty. We had to find homes for many of the animals, but a few we were able to release into the wild without fear of their destruction either from man or from an inability to look after themselves. Duckie, the gannet, was the first to go. He was by that time a fine and powerful bird, and although still in immature plumage, well equipped to fend for himself. We had taught him to feed himself by placing his fish in a large polythene basin full of water so that he had to stab at his food with his sabre bill, then juggle the fish round until its head was pointing down his gullet, then, with a flick of his head, land it in the back of his throat. This was followed by the comical up and down swallowing action until his crop bulged and he was ready for the next one.

Duckie had been kept in an open pen not big enough to permit the long flapping take-off gannets require to rise from the land, and so we had no cause to clip his wings. They were long and pointed and immaculately preened. That day we carried him, squawking and protesting vociferously, to the highest point of the island. To the west the land sloped away sharply to the sea twenty yards below us. There we waited for a gust of wind, since we wished to give Duckie every possible chance of success in what was probably only his second flight. (The first having been little more than a glide from his cliff-edge nest to the sea.) At last the moment came, and with a mighty heave Donald cast the protesting bird up above our heads and into the eye of the wind. It was an anxious moment. Duckie's wings seemed to be glued to his sides as he rose into the air. Then, as he felt himself falling, they shot out like great swords from either side and carved into the rushing air. A cumbersome bundle of protesting feathers was instantly transformed into a bird. No captive bird this, but a wild gannet ready to soar and glide, dip and dive into the fish-full sea. Duckie flew as if he had been flying for years with strong, shallow thrusts of his wings and long graceful glides. He never looked back. Within seconds he was a speck against the grey islands along the horizon and, just before he was lost from our view, we saw him sweep low over the waves and pitch effortlessly on the sea. We returned to the headland three times that day and scanned the water and the sky for sign of him, but he had accepted his liberty and gone.

The herons, too, were to have their freedom. Now that there were no foxes on the island it was safe to allow them to go free; they were to potter and fish in the tidal bays and wade knee-deep among the weed in search of prey. Their release held no anxiety but was no less a delight. We carefully unfastened one side of their wire pen and retired to watch them discover their freedom for themselves.

All four birds were unable to fly since we had clipped the primary feathers of their wings, but new feathers were growing fast and it would be only a short while before they regained full powers of flight. One by one they approached the gap in the wire and peered at it in comical bewilderment.

For a while they seemed unable to acept the situation. As if some invisible barrier still remained, they stalked back and forth along where the wire had been. Suddenly, as if by accident, one bird stepped into the gap. It stopped abruptly, clearly astonished by its own boldness, and then it was through, out on to the path leading to the lighthouse bay.

An hour later all four herons were in the bay, paddling happily from pool to pool, stabbing eagerly at a darting goby here and staring glassily at others beyond their reach. They looked as happy and as pleased as it is possible for a heron to look, and we saw reflected in their liberty a brief glimpse of our former plans. That bay was to have been the enclosure for the herons and waders and they were behaving then exactly as they would have done had our zoo project succeeded.

This business of hand-rearing animals and later returning them to the wild is not as simple as it may appear, and is not something to be entered into lightly. It has been and is still being done all too frequently with everything from foxes to flamingoes, and usually with disastrous results.

In the early stages of their lives animals go through a period vital to the success of their later life during which a process which behaviourists have called 'imprinting' takes place. That is to say, the animal's brain is imprinted with the sights, sounds and smells of its own environment and parental species. During this period a fox-cub learns that it is a fox and a flamingo chick that it is a flamingo. If, at this vital point, the young animal is removed from its natural parents and environment, there is a strong chance that it will grow up thinking it is something other than it really is. A classical experiment was carried out a few years ago by a now famous behaviourist team which involved a brood of chicks. The first thing that the chicks saw as soon as they emerged from the incubator was a large red balloon. The balloon was made to move by means of a piece of string and the chicks immediately accepted it as their parent. At a later stage

when the imprinting process was complete the genuine
mother hen was returned to the chicks, but her brood were
not interested. They toddled pathetically along behind the
balloon and nestled up to it whenever it stopped. In his
recent book *The Human Zoo*, Dr Desmond Morris has
called this process 'mal-imprinting', and it is the mal-
imprinting of young animals fostered by well-meaning
humans which concerns us here.

Our natural (or paternal) instinct attracts us all to the
young of most animals, but particularly to warm and furry
mammals. The response to kittens and puppies is typical and,
all too often, when we come across the young of wild animals
we are similarly aroused and tempted to adopt the wildling
in the same manner. For a few weeks everything is fine and
then, all of a sudden, the animal is no longer the cuddly
thing it was before but an adult animal outwardly portray-
ing the characteristics of its species; fox cubs start to smell
strongly and want to be nocturnal; badger cubs dig up the
herbaceous border and set musk on objects all round the
house (which to them is their territory); birds start to fly
about and are invariably messy. At this point the problems
become too great and often an attempt is made to 'return it
to the wild'. One hears of animals being taken off in the car
to some lonely spot and given their liberty and the success
of their release is later boasted in blissful ignorance. I wonder how many such successful releases really mean that the
creature wandered off bewildered and afraid in its new and
savage environment and perished through starvation, predation or rejection by its own species.

Just because a 'tamed' animal appears to be able to look
after itself, it does not mean that it is capable of existing in
a wild state. Dr Morris tells us in his book that the enormous
difficulties experienced in mating zoo animals are often a
direct result of mal-imprinting. Hand-reared monkeys and
chimpanzees only want to mate with their human foster
species, and the same is the case with dogs which have been
removed from their litters too young and continually em-

barrass their owners or their guests by trying to copulate with them. Such dogs are mal-imprinted; they believe that they are human, and they may never mate successfully with another dog. This applies to wild adoptees in exactly the same way. When the released fox or squirrel or hedgehog or jackdaw goes off so happily into the woods it may well be instinctively equipped to feed itself; but it is at best condemned to celibacy and it is far more likely to perish at the hand of some human it was reared to accept as a friend.

It was, then, with some forethought and caution that our wildlings had been reared and, as was later necessary, released. Duckie was already a fully fledged and therefore a fully imprinted gannet before we took him in, and our only concern was that he should be able to feed himself. The herons, too, were fully imprinted herons when they came to the island; and although they were not afraid of us, we had not attempted to handle them and I was certain they would quickly revert to a completely wild state once they were finding food for themselves and no longer dependent upon humans. Owl, on the other hand, was a text-book example of a mal-imprinted animal who had no idea that he was a bird, least of all an owl. Even if his wing had mended and he had been able to fly we could never have released him. Instead we were faced with the problem of finding a new home for him, and one whose owner was well acquainted with the works of Chaucer. Thankfully this did not prove difficult and Owl was dispatched in a cardboard box to Devonshire where he was re-adopted by a man who had recently lost a tame tawny owl and who possessed an enviable Chaucerian vocabulary. Owl is now a happy and contented mal-imprinted owl.

Crowlin, our carrion crow, was a borderline case and it was doubtful whether he would have been able to exist in the wild as a normal crow should; but, like Owl, Crowlin's release was not a practical proposition – at least not from a humanitarian viewpoint. To have released Crowlin would

have been an invitation to anybody out with a gun to score
an easy kill. Like the hoodies, carrion crows are, rightly or
wrongly, shot on sight in the Highlands and any bird as
unafraid of man as was Crowlin would have lasted only a
matter of hours.

Crowlin was essentially Donald's pet and it was therefore
fitting that Donald was able to keep him. They left together,
the bird on Donald's shoulder and occasionally on his head,
as they crossed the ferry to the railway station at Kyle. Now,
twelve months later, I learn that Donald is no longer boss in
his own home. The vociferous Crowlin has adopted him,
his house and garden with that indomitable impudence
characteristic of all the crow family.

There remained only the domestic stock, the ram and the
two goats, and Teko the old Camusfeàrna otter and his com-
panions from those sunlit days, the deer-hounds Hazel and
Dirk. The ram and the goats are domesticated still, but on
fresh Skye pastures, and the old deer-hounds are retired to a
new life in the distinguished company of other elderly
hounds. Teko alone chose not to be moved again. He died
suddenly and unexpectedly of a heart attack whilst swimming in his pool. We buried him at the foot of a huge boulder
at the top of the island and I carved his name and dates in
the rock face above the spot : *TEKO* 1959–69. A memorial
to the last of the *Ring of Bright Water* otters.

As the dinghy crunched into the shingle of Kyleakin beach
for the last time on that December morning, we turned to
look back at the island which had been our home. The scene
was of grey and white. The pale grey sea at our feet reflected the snow-heavy greyness of the sky; and the lighthouse and the long, low house alone stood white against an
interminable grey beyond. Behind us the gaunt Skye hills
rose darkly to their snow line, its whiteness indistinguishable
in the dense cloud which swirled heavily around their peaks.
A bitter wind swept in from the sea snatching white crests
from the waves, and a band of surf for a moment engulfed
the island, ringing it round in a sweeping white embrace. A

small party of gulls pitched effortlessly on the sea in front of the eider island; five white specks rising and falling in the swell. For the first time I saw a good reason for the island's name, Eilean Bhan, the White Island.

Lewis Grassic Gibbon

His famous trilogy, *A Scots Quair*

Sunset Song 70p

Chris Guthrie knew love and hate in the same breath. Hate for the ceaseless toil of a life in the Mearns that brought her mother to tragic despair . . . Love for the tumbling land of her heritage – a love shared by Ewan, with whom she finds ecstatic union . . .

Cloud Howe 60p

Married again, now to Robert Colquohoun, minister, Chris sets out on a new life, with new hopes . . .

As industrial strife and class struggle bring violence and discontent to the lively, bustling community of Segget, so Fate brings devastating changes to her life.

Grey Granite 60p

Living in a new world of factories, pubs, strikes, marches, riots, tanner hops, picture-houses and picket lines, Chris's hopes for the future lie in the burning love between her son Ewan and Ellen Johns – a love as tempestuous as the times . . .

The Steel Bonnets 95p
George MacDonald Fraser
The story of the Anglo-Scottish Border Reivers

Armstrong Beattie Bell Burn Charlton Collingwood Croser Dacre Dodd Elliot Fenwick Forster Graham Hall Hetherington Hume Irvine Johnstone Kerr Laidlaw Little Lowther Maxwell Milburn Musgrave Nixon Pringle Ridley Robson Rutherford Routledge Scott Storey Tait Trotter Turnbull

Were your ancestors among the great raiding families from the six counties on either side of the Border Marches?

George MacDonald Fraser, creator of the 'Flashman' sagas, has produced an immensely entertaining and informative portrait of the guerrillas in steel bonnets.

'A remarkably successful book on a fascinating subject, well organized and well written' TIMES LITERARY SUPPLEMENT

Selected bestsellers

☐ **Jaws** Peter Benchley 70p
☐ **Let Sleeping Vets Lie** James Herriot 60p
☐ **It Shouldn't Happen to a Vet** James Herriot 60p
☐ **Vet In Harness** James Herriot 60p
☐ **Tinker Tailor Soldier Spy** John le Carré 60p
☐ **Alive: The Story of the Andes Survivors** (illus) Piers Paul
   Read 75p
☐ **Gone with the Wind** Margaret Mitchell £1.50
☐ **Mandingo** Kyle Onstott 75p
☐ **Shout at the Devil** Wilbur Smith 70p
☐ **Cashelmara** Susan Howatch £1.25
☐ **Hotel** Arthur Hailey 80p
☐ **The Tower** Richard Martin Stern 70p
   (filmed as *The Towering Inferno*)
☐ **Bonecrack** Dick Francis 60p
☐ **Jonathan Livingston Seagull** Richard Bach 80p
☐ **The Fifth Estate** Robin Moore 75p
☐ **Royal Flash** George MacDonald Fraser 60p
☐ **The Nonesuch** Georgette Heyer 60p
☐ **Murder Most Royal** Jean Plaidy 80p
☐ **The Grapes of Wrath** John Steinbeck 95p

All these books are available at your bookshop or newsagent;
or can be obtained direct from the publisher
Just tick the titles you want and fill in the form below
Prices quoted are applicable in UK

Pan Books, Cavaye Place, London SW10 9PG
Send purchase price plus 15p for the first book and 5p for each
additional book, to allow for postage and packing

Name (block letters)_____

Address_____

_____

While every effort is made to keep prices low, it is sometimes
necessary to increase prices at short notice. Pan Books reserve the
right to show on covers new retail prices which may differ from
those advertised in the text or elsewhere